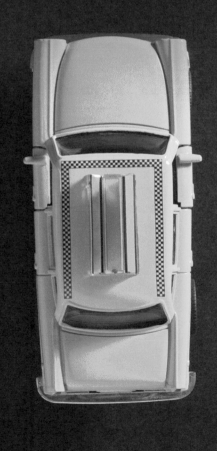

The MIND TRIP Game

Play Your Way to Conscious Thinking

Audrey Newmont

Balboa Press books may be ordered through booksellers or by contacting:

Balboa Press
A Division of Hay House
1663 Liberty Drive
Bloomington, IN 47403
www.balboapress.com
1 (877) 407-4847

ISBN: 978-1-9822-4418-7 (sc)
ISBN: 978-1-9822-4419-4 (e)

Library of Congress Control Number: 2020904940

Print information available on the last page.

Balboa Press rev. date: 12/11/2024

THE ADVENTURE BEGINS HERE

To weather the upcoming storms of life, the people who will survive and thrive are those who can be resilient, adapt, and change. Many of us who are in our forties and older may recognize this more than the later generations who are coming up. We did not have cell phones, we had to learn about the Internet and all the new technology that comes with the twenty-first century. In the past, we received news daily in the form of newspapers and TV. Now it is a continual onslaught of many types of news and information. This comes with its own problems with determining what is real and keeping up with the massive amount of information.

In our youth, we did not have as much violence and terrorism, the storms were not as devastating, and we did not have to contend with worrying about the food that we ate, the air we breathe, or the excessive energy that we're feeling. In many ways, life was simpler than it is now. Anxiety, depression, and stress were not as prevalent, and now, along with too many adults, even our children are anxiety ridden.

I have had to adapt my own life in ways that I never dreamed would happen. I can say that there are too many ways that I've "been there, done that." I have overcome a lot of painful challenges that hurt myself and the ones I have loved, never understanding why or how I created the pain. My own level of dysfunction was fine when I was single, but it certainly did not work for me when I became a mother. I had to be a better person to be a better Mom for my daughter.

I have to say that my experience definitely had its massive ups and downs. My intention for writing this book was to pass on the information and wisdom I gained along the way, in a manner I wish I could have learned. I purposefully made it simple and effective so that you could easily use the tools and get through your challenging "stuff" as soon as possible. As you will see in the book with the personal stories I tell, there is a reason why it took me ten long years just to sort through all the material I've learned. The foundation of my spiritual growth was in the teachings of Ernest Holmes and Rev. Michael Beckwith at Agape International Spiritual Center, where I became a spiritual practitioner. My training to become a hypnotherapist was at the Hypnosis Motivation Institute. It was the foundation of my mental growth.

I have studied various teachers of science of the mind, metaphysical anatomy and function of the body, and Quantum Intelligence from experts like Dr. Bruce Lipton, Gregg Braden, Lynne McTaggart, Dr. Joe Dispenza, etc. Also, some of my most beloved teachers have been channeled. Paul Selig with the Guides, Ester Hicks with Abraham, Golden Arrow through Alexandra, and of course Merlin through my husband Nick Newmont. This information has been the glue that has brought the spiritual and mental to a deeper understanding of who I truly am and how I make my human experience better.

I am beyond grateful to all the teachers over all these years, the information and wisdom they put into form have helped develop me into the person who I am today. Owing to those who I have led the way; I can share my process with a new unique and playful approach. My deepest appreciation to all the authors listed in the quotes throughout the book, your words have been my greatest inspiration and have literally saved my life.

Working with so many people over the years has allowed me to fine-tune the information that I share in a way that is simple, easy to understand, effective, and fast. Once you learn the process of how the game goes, it usually takes about twenty-one days to change a belief or habit, the more you stick with it and commit yourself to use the tools, the better your life will get.

Here is a suggestion, let's declare today a new clean slate, a new starting point for *you*! This new game that you are about to play is an opportunity to make life a bit more agreeable, more passionate, and freer. This is not to say that life will be without challenges—we all have our moments. You are about to learn more about your unconscious thinking and how to change it, how to communicate more effectively, how to use your timeline to learn about your challenging patterns and own the process of changing them. You are about to get off the victimization loop and take responsibility for your life. You will be creating more balance, understanding, and using your energy in an intentional way. On this adventure you will learn how to move *through* the difficult moments in life and not get stuck in them.

Now, onto the business of learning a new kind of game.

THE GAME OF YOUR LIFE

Do you ever notice that when people are playing games, they do whatever it takes to win? They learn the rules and lead with determination and a passion, which is extremely focused and direct. Think about the people in your life, maybe yourself. Do you know anyone who does not play some sort of game like cards or Monopoly? Online games such as Xbox, WII, Words with Friends? The gaming world takes up a lot of time, and it can be a huge distraction from our individual lives. Many gamers play online games with more drive and intention than they used to in the moments of day-to-day life.

This mind game is designed to bring that kind of energy and drive you back to the focus of your real life. You get to be a gamer in a new way … to play to win at your own experiences. You get to level up happiness, health, peace, abundance, success, and love!

As you read further, you will get the details of how to play. For now, as a foundation of where you are going in this book, know that you will be taking a "Road Trip." You will learn how to use the "Game Board" that is your road map. You will have a "Token," that is a car that represents you, and the "Tools" are what you use to transform your life in an immensely powerful way. All of these directives are designed to put the conscious YOU into the driver's seat and get you to your best destinations.

All the information and activities that you are about to get into are designed to restructure new pathways in your brain, to pay attention to and use your feelings, and to begin a new way to get to where you really want to go and how you want to be along the way.

You have heard of people going on a "road trip," by getting in a car and going on an adventure. *This game is a road trip for your mind.* The intention is to get into the roadways within your mind and process a change in the way you think. Therefore, intentionally creating your new life. For many people, the road trip is often out of control—we do things we do not want to do, we go places we do not want to go, we run out of gas, or we break down.

This game is designed to help you understand where you have been, why you were there, what you want, and how to get it. There are points in the book where you are invited to take a Mind Trip. The more you do these exercises, the quicker you change old limiting habits and beliefs. This is where the magic happens.

Be on the lookout for these prompts throughout the book.

MIND ROAD TRIP FOR:

- 🚗 Mapping the Journey
- 🚗 Perspective
- 🚗 Mind Road Trip for Mind/Brain Chatter
- 🚗 Mind Road Trip for Expansion
- 🚗 Dumping the Trunk
- 🚗 Generating Resilience
- 🚗 Focus on Future Tripping
- 🚗 Increasing Clarity
- 🚗 Letting Go
- 🚗 Resilience
- 🚗 Getting Off the Loop
- 🚗 Connecting
- 🚗 Relationships
- 🚗 Visioning
- 🚗 Alignment and Balance

TERMS OF ENGAGEMENT FOR GAME PLAY

These are some "Rules of the Road." Just as we have actual laws that we follow with regard to actually driving on the road. These rules are with the same intention to keep us all getting to our destination safely, on purpose, and enjoying the trip along the way.

Really think about each as you read them, highlight the ones that might be challenging.

As you move forward with this book you will be acquiring new tools that will help to address any challenge and work through it.

* Be deliberate and on purpose.
* Know what you want. Don't "no" what you do want.
* Use every challenge as an opportunity to move up the board.
* Keep focused on any-and-all solutions.
* Have fun!
* Appreciate anything and everything.
* Be patient with yourself. This is a process, not an overnight miracle.
* Ask if you are not sure. There are answers.
* Be compassionate with yourself and others. We are all just trying to figure it out.
* Own your words, they are creative but can be destructive.
* Be intentional, honest, thoughtful, and considerate.
* Focus on any and all good news.
* Hold bad news in your affirmative prayers.
* Keep moving up the emotional ladder, moving toward feeling better.
* Put yourself first as much as possible, and then be of service to others.
* Say "no" when you want to … nicely, and with a smile.
* Keep challenging yourself and adding to the "Do This" suggestions.
* No shoving your emotions down, be authentic with your feelings.
* Follow your intuition.
* Look for anything to inspire you.
* Be mighty and *brave*.
* Know right action is always taking place, trust life's process, and have faith.
* Make your own additions to this list.

The Game Token

This is a very important part of the game, as this token will represent you.

In the set up for playing, imagine your perfect car ... In your mind, pick any car that works for you. It could be any type. Choose one that you are comfortable with, that you feel special in, and that is reliable. That car you have imagined is going to represent your *Body*.

Your human body is a complex system of many moving parts, and it contains energy and awareness. The main job your car/body provides is to get you from here to there and allow you the ability to experience all that life has to offer. It is not who you are, but what allows you to be who you are.

The driver of the car is your *Soul*. As the driver, it will represent your character in this game. Your Soul is your connection to experience love, intelligence, creativity, inspiration, beauty, and light. It is what makes the body alive and vibrant. Your Soul is the best and highest expression of you. Your Soul is the place where the intelligent universe downloads.

DRIVING LESSONS

Under the heading of, "I swear, you just can't make this stuff up ...." I am sitting in my office working on this very part of the book. From my floor-to-ceiling windows, I notice there is a car that keeps driving around the building. It is Sunday, so not very many people are here—and it caught my attention. Turns out that it is a kid in a driving lesson with his father! Perfect!

Do you remember when you learned how to drive? Were you scared at first? How about having to learn all the controls of the car, the rules of the road, having to pay attention to the other drivers on the road, and figuring out where you were going—all at the same time!

Think about how you are now, you know your destination and you get in the car. You do not have to think about how to turn on the car, hit the brakes, push the gas, maybe you don't pay attention to the other drivers as much as you used to, the rules of the road don't even come into your conscious awareness, and you are on auto pilot with the controls. How many times have you driven past an exit or gotten to your location only to realize that you do not even remember driving there! Think about all of that, and what you are about to read the next time you get in the car.

When driving, many people spend a lot of time looking into the rear-view mirror feeling regret, blame, shame, anger, etc. We remember what other people have done to us, what we have done to them. We lament choices that we wished we had made differently. We stay in the grief of loved ones lost, and what we could or should have done to keep them. You may be thinking, "Why did I do that"? "Why did I allow someone to do that to me." "If I had done things differently my life would have been different, and I would have been happier, richer, or more successful." The list of how we can beat ourselves up goes on, and when we stay in the pain of the past, it is almost impossible to move forward. We are literally stuck in a space that does not exist anymore. You are in a loop … past trauma that is still driving the car. Think about the side view mirror, the one that can be distorted? Do you look back at your past and make it even worse than it was?

When you are engaged in viewing life through those mirrors, you're not in present in the now moment in your car. This lack of attention to the moment can cause you to hit the car in front of you or take the wrong turn down the hill to your worst nightmares. If you do choose to spend time considering the past, the most beneficial way to do that would be to remember with more understanding, compassion, and love. Allow the memories to light up your heart.

Another thing we are prone to do while driving is to look too far into the future and think something terrifying like, "What if I get cancer, what if they leave me, what if I get fired, etc." At this moment, none of these things have happened, but we are thinking about the possibility of these tragedies and looking way down the road as if they might happen. We see it in our minds eye, and we feel the anxiety, worry, terror and fear as if it were real. While facilitating a rehab group in Malibu, one of the clients informed me that this is known as "future tripping."

Think about your life, be honest with yourself, and notice how much time you are present? How much time spent in the rear-view mirror or future tripping? The most powerful place to be is in the moment, looking out the windows of your eyes and being present to what is happening right now. In this moment owning an intention and perception that is in alignment with who you choose to be and where you want to go.

Interesting fact, your feelings create much of your experience in life. Remember I said it was an energy powered car? One of the ways that you use your energy to power the car is through heartfelt feelings. When you feel, you program into the navigational system to where you are going. When you worry, have anxiety and stress about something in the future it can create consequences that you do not really want.

Those feelings and the thoughts attached will make you drive yourself right to that which you fear the most. I am afraid I'll lose my job, or my partner, or I won't get whatever … I have seen it happen all the time, I'm sure you have too. This is one of the big reasons why you may want to pay attention to how you are driving. More about this will come up later in this book. For now, pay attention, be aware of how much you are present. For those of us that are challenged on how to be present, here are tips on how to be present.

- ∞ Pay attention to your body. If you're feeling funky you might be feeling guilty, sad, remorseful or regret something difficult that happened in the past, or you may be anxious, worried, or stressed about a possible future.
- ∞ Notice your thoughts, are your focused on the solutions of life or the problems?
- ∞ Be aware of your actions. Sometimes we will be knee deep in something before we realize that it's not working for us. REALIGN! Get back in the driver's seat and adjust to this moment. It's like you took a detour, now back to conscious driving. No judgement!

When we are not present, looking at the past or possible future, we might not see a pothole in the road. Imagine that the pothole is filled with mud, and it get splashed on your windows and you are not able to see clearly. That is when you use the Fear Into Power tool coming up in the book. Imagine that tool is your windshield wipers, and you will be able to see more clearly and move from your panic to your patience, from anxiety to calm, anger to composed, etc.

This part about the windshield wipers came up in a group that I was leading as I was telling this car analogy. One of the group members said, "But Audrey what if I move from my fear to my power, and I still have a film on my windshield, and I can't get it off? I did not miss a beat, I looked at him and said, "Oh that's when you need windshield wiper fluid and that's me!"

Sometimes we do need help from someone to see more clearly. Be brave, ask for directions! Find someone that makes sense to you and let them share their wisdom and knowledge to help you see with more clarity.

What is in your trunk? What have you been carrying around for years and years? As you are going around the board of your life you want to start eliminating that extra baggage that's weighing you down and not allowing you to go as fast as you want in your life. Make a commitment to yourself to look at that baggage and allow yourself the grace to let it go with ease. By baggage, I mean the old hurts we hold on to, past trauma, painful memories, etc. You know the stuff; we all have some. This is one of the parts to this game that is a process, you are not going to clean out the trunk overnight. You can start with the lighter less painful memories and build up to the more challenging feelings. Be patient and compassionate with yourself, those things did not show up overnight, it takes a little while to gently pull them out. The tools shared in this book will help, keep reading.

How are you taking care of your engine? We need to put in fuel that is able to be processed by the car. Put in in the highest-level energy into your body to get the kind of power that you want. That means eating organic, GMO free and a lot of foods that have been touched by the sun firsthand. Make sure you are keeping a balance. Your engine is a fine machine, it requires maintenance and tender loving care. Find your support crew! My husband Nick and I have a team of holistic practitioners who have been amazing at getting us on track with much better health and greater energy to do all the many things we do. Sometimes your beautiful car is going to need to go through the car wash and be a little pampered and shine up. It feels good to get the grime off and sparkle sometimes. Yes?

Let us think about the lights on the front of the car, in moments of darkness, which I believe most of us have, we must be able to see more clearly. If you are having one of those dark moments of the soul, turn up the light by using meditation and visualization (two of the Tools for Transformation). It is not a bad idea to pull off to the side and take a moment to be calm and find clarity before driving forward. Another thing that you can do at this moment is take a pit stop. When race car drivers take a pit stop, they have a whole crew that makes sure that they are in optimal condition to get back into the race. Find your crew, let them support you in the challenging dark moments. Also, be a crew member for others, be of service, it earns you extra gas credits.

Do you have kids in your car? They are sitting in the backseat and watching you … every single minute, watching you drive. They are learning how to drive their car by observing you. We can tell kids many things, but they learn more from the observation and copying, than by what we say. So be truly clear, while you're "driving" daily, your kids are learning how to drive through you. They learn your habits, speech, mannerisms, beliefs. They learn how to value and love themselves and others through you. Think about it, how do you think you learned how to run your life? Do you find yourself doing things that are the spitting image of your parents? In the areas of your love life, financial and health do you have similarities with your family?

Who's in your passenger seat? Is this the person you want to be having the grand adventure of life with? Does this person fill your car with love and laughter? Is the person you hold the closest giving you good directions? Are they distracting you from your driving? Are they supportive while you are driving? There will be people coming in and out of your passenger seat for the duration of your life. You are going to give them a ride for a minute or a lifetime. With the information you are about to learn you will choose those people wisely, and make sure that they are in alignment with you.

As you are going around the board of your life there's going to be other cars on the road that you'll have to deal with. It is important to know how to be a defensive driver and stay clear of the people who are weaving all over the road with no purpose, or worse, those with malicious intentions who are wreaking havoc. It is possible to circumvent those drivers much of the time.

As you are moving forward there will be road signs along the way. Pay attention, an unexpected detour can take you to the best places! Notice the signs along the way, drive accordingly. The Universe is telling you something. You may go over construction zones as life hits a challenging moment; slow down and take the time to be present with what is going on. Use this opportunity to be reflective and take care of personal business. Think about when you're driving and there is the sign that says, "temporary inconvenience, permanent improvement.

Appreciate those moments of clear sailing with open fields of possibilities in front of you. Being appreciative is the foot on the gas, you will make the greatest possibilities happen with that kind of energy on the intention. It is like putting jet fuel in your tank!

So, we know that the Soul is the core of you, that is the driver of the car. It is also humanness that makes the key decisions on what we "Be" in any given minute. For this game consider that you have three avatars that are in the "driver's seat." Here's how you know which aspect of you is driving the car in the present moment.

Driver #3 The Inner Child, the one running an unconscious autopilot driven by fear.

- Out on an extended "road trip"
- Conditional, Uncertain and Restricted
- Too focused on "Selfies" in the rearview mirror
- Too easy to anger
- Habitually Worrying
- Living with Addictions
- Driving in circles, back to old patterns
- Lots of drama and trauma
- Being anywhere but present
- Looking to the future with worry, dread, anxiety

The #2 Driver, the Adult, the conscious driver with logic, reasoning,

- Have Intention Set
- Be Present, Live in the Moment
- Focused on Destination
- Living Unconditionally, Clear and Free
- Certainty/Faith is a habit
- Make Healthy Choices
- Know Calm is a Choice
- Overcome Roadblocks with Purpose
- Focus on Solutions

You are the one that's designing the road in front of you. This is your game, your life, and you have this opportunity to develop it the way you want, not the way you learned from your parents and other influences. The adult you has a good plan for your life, she/he knows the best and highest for each moment. Let them drive with determined intention. Also, listen to your passenger in the back and learn from what they want to share with you in times of anxiety, stress, anger and sadness. I have had many conversations with my little Audi in the backseat. Once I understand the reason for the "feels" and I am on to the solution, I tell Audi, "no more back seat driving, I'll get us there safely, we'll have fun, and you can relax." Then, I am able to get back to being the adult with the fun kid in the backseat as much as possible,

THE UNIVERSE IS YOUR CO-PILOT

You've met the first two drivers, now for some conversation about what I call the "#1 Driver". We are all connected to something much greater than all the greatness we can possibly imagine. As you understand the connection you have with grand intelligence and then use that connection intentionally, then you are lined up on the highway of life with all cylinders blasting with rocket fuel. Let's take a look at what that means.

"Through the connection that joins all things, scientists have shown that the "stuff" that the universe is made of—waves and particles of energy—responds and conforms to the expectations, judgments and beliefs that we create about our world.

In a world where an intelligent field of energy connects everything from global peace to personal healing, what may have sounded like fantasy and miracles in the past suddenly becomes possible in our lives. There is one small catch, however.

Our power to change our bodies and our world is dormant until we awaken it. The key to awakening such an awesome power is that have to make a small shift in the way we see ourselves in the universe. We must see ourselves as a part of everything, rather than separate from everything. Beyond merely thinking of ourselves from this unified view, we must feel ourselves as part of all that we experience. With this one little shift in perception, we are given access to the most powerful force in the universe, and the key to address even the seemingly impossible situations in our lives." ~Gregg Braden

Intelligent Creative *Energy* powers and drives the car (your body). This energy goes through the car, as the car, all the time. It is intelligent energy because it reacts to you, and once you have an awareness of how to use your energy intentionally you will have the ability to use that energy to move your car in the direction that you determine. The more you become of aware of and open to this energy, the more powerfully you get to use it to move your car forward in the game.

Your energy is the powerful force that creates the dynamic miraculous experience of your life. This knowledge has been one of the most important things that I have learned, it has been the "thing" that has given me the ability to lead the life that I'm so grateful for now.

Modern science has proven that there is a field of energy that is present everywhere, in and as all things. Scientists recognize that this energy is intelligent and interactive with us, as us. It is you; it is me, the expanded WE. We are connected in this field of energy just as much as certain plants are connected in the soil of the earth. Much of the time we do not "feel" this energy or connection, but that doesn't mean that it's not there.

This energy is called many names, some of my favorite terms are Infinite Intelligence, Unified Field, Source, Source Energy, and as one of my favorite teachers likes to call it, the Divine Matrix. Many people call It God.

"There is an intelligence that's giving you life that's always present and many people don't take the time to connect with by being present." ~Dr. Joe Dispenza

As you get further into this book you will learn to use that connection to improve your relationships, your abundance, your health, your intuition, your consciousness and even your intelligence.

SUPERCHARGED INTELLIGENCE

Think of your body like it is the smartest smart car ever! You are a space where the intelligence and energy of the Universe comes through. You are expansive. You are intelligent, and you create with, in union, connected to ALL that Is.

"The true nature of myself is the wholeness of the Universe." ~Deepak Chopra

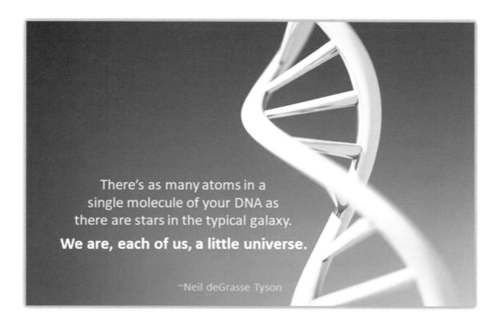

There's as many atoms in a single molecule of your DNA as there are stars in the typical galaxy.
We are, each of us, a little universe.

~Neil deGrasse Tyson

"The chemicals that make up a cell also share a field of information. It's that invisible field of information that orchestrates the hundreds of thousands of functions of the cell at any given second. Scientists are beginning to realize that a field of information exists that's responsible for myriad cellular functions existing beyond the boundaries of matter. It's this invisible field of consciousness that orchestrates all of the functions of the cells, tissues, organs, and systems of the body. How do certain chemicals and molecules of your cells know what to do and interact with such precision? There's an energetic field surrounding the cell that's the summation of energy from atoms, molecules, and chemicals working together in balance that gives birth to matter, and it's that vital field of information that matter draws from."

~Joe Dispenza, You Are the Placebo: Making Your Mind Matter

You are absolutely a miracle of life! Here is how incredibly miraculous *You* are, think about this, your human body knows exactly how to function. It is all intelligent energy that makes all these things happen, the Universe is working with you in so many ways. Think about these things.

- ★ You do not have to tell yourself to digest food or to breathe the air.
- ★ You do not have to tell your muscles to tighten up to do the tasks of life.
- ★ You do not have to tell your cells to divide or your heart to beat.
- ★ You do not have to tell your liver to cleanse your blood or all the rest of your organs to do the beautiful dance of life in your beautiful body.
- ★ You do not have to tell your body to heal a wound and much more.
- ★ You do not have to tell your body to procreate.

I have a power statement that I use all the time, "The Universe moves through me as me, and divine right action is taking place." I am letting that #1 Driver know that I trust that all my good is happening. I'm setting a road map.

Now that you know who your "drivers" are, you are ready to go! It's time to learn how to play your way to conscious intention using the game board.

GAME BOARD, THE ROUTE TO EMPOWERMENT

You have the token that now needs a board to level up with. This is your path to take every time you have a challenge/problem, a feeling that is difficult or painful, or you're stuck. The more you take this path, the more you get to level up and own the full dynamic of your life.

As you can see from the GAMEBOARD photo below, the board is straightforward, easy to remember and simple to use. But don't be fooled by the simplicity, it's designed to help you go deep into the unconscious crap that sabotages the best and highest happening in life.

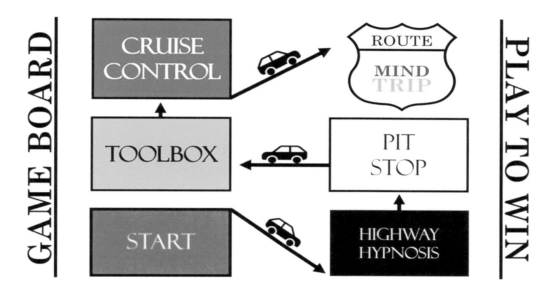

"You are the master of your destiny. You can influence, direct and control your own environment. You can make your life what you want it to be." ~Napoleon Hill

"Do not wait: the time will never be 'just right'. Start where you stand, and work whatever tools you may have at your command and better tools will be found as you go along." ~Napoleon Hill

WHAT IS YOUR INTENTION?

START

What do you want?

Be specific, detailed, deliberate and focused.

Your intention determines where you go and how you get there.

INTENTION LEADS THE WAY

When you get in your car to go somewhere, you almost always know where you are going. It is your intention to go to work, to visit friends, your home, shopping, or possibly out of town. Usually there is no doubt in your mind that you will arrive at your destination, and many times while you are getting there you might not even be paying attention to your driving. Your mind is focused on the stuff of the day, and you are on autopilot.

When driving your car in this game, you must know where you are going, or you'll be driving around aimlessly in the direction of the unconscious fears that you're feeling.

Intention is what programs where you are going to into the navigational system. You can have an intention to have a great loving partner, or more abundance, or maybe an intention to just be happier.

Your intention generates the map that is the guide to your destination.

I've had many people that I've worked with in my practice that have not been clear on an intention that they want for themselves. They just can't think of anything and finally it comes down to the question of, "Do you just want to be happier?" It could look just like that. It doesn't have to be a concrete defined goal like getting a new home, love interest or more money, in fact sometimes just being happier really affects a lot of the other things along the way.

MIND ROAD TRIP TO MAP THE JOURNEY

To know your intention, ask yourself these questions and take the time to write them down.

- What do you want in this moment in your life?
- Think about your health, joy, success/abundance, or just being in love.
- Which of these areas of your life need some good direction?
- Are you willing to create a happier life for yourself?
- What will it take for you to get there?
- Are you willing to do that?
- What is your best plan of action?

Write down at least three things that you would like to accomplish in the next month. Make them reasonable and important to you. The next thing to do is, wait for it …

Something difficult and challenging is going to happen and you will feel one or more of the following feelings/emotions.

FRUSTRATED	APPREHENSIVE	RESENTFUL
EMBARRASSED	FRIGHTENED	DISGUSTED
UNEASY	JEALOUS	ANNOYED
WORRIED	UNNERVED	DISAPPOINTED
AFRAID	MAD	ASHAMED
TERRIFIED	ANGRY	OVERWHELMED
NERVOUS	EXASPERATED	APATHETIC
PANICKY	FURIOUS	DISCOURAGED
JITTERY	HOSTILE	DEPRESSED
HORRIFIED	BITTER	ENRAGED
ANXIOUS	PESSIMISTTIC	HOPELESS
LONELY	LONELY	UNWORTHY
SUSPICIOUS	DESPERATE	

When these feelings are happening consider yourself in HIGHWAY HYPNOSIS.

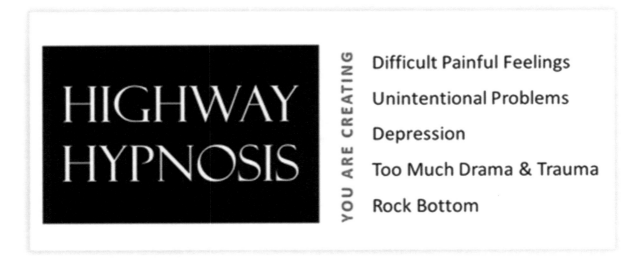

This is GO time in the game. When you recognize that you're feeling bad, it's alright. No judgement on anything. Those difficult feelings are just one of those unconscious mindmaps that you are running. Your feelings can be the greatest guide to your self empowerment. The good news is that when you have the ability to recognize your feelings, you get to do something about them. You don't have to just be in the anger, frustration, anxiety or fear and be victim to it. You, my friend go into the power seat as soon as you are able to identify that your feeling bad.

Be kind to yourself for feelings that have been supressed for a long period of time. They aren't meant to be resolved in one big moment, allow for them to come up with ease, and as you can handle them. Especially the feelings of grief, they are some of the most challenging. In this moment, consider that you are creating more safety and you're managing your emotional life in a new constructive way.

Now that you have recognized your feelings, you get to move up the Board to take a PIT STOP.

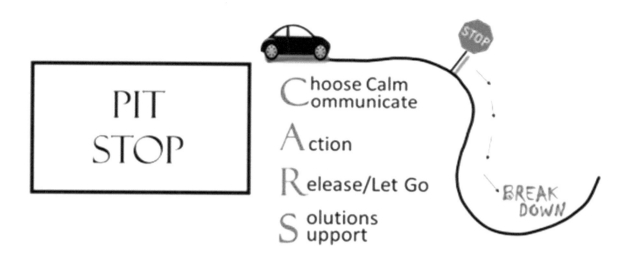

This is your PIT STOP at the top of the hill. You know you have the fear feeling, before it turns into something uncontrollable, stop the car! This is one of the main parts of the board, this is where you check yourself before you go too far down that slippery slope of rage, stress, worry and anxiety, deep into rock bottom, stop yourself as best you can! One of my favorite things to do in that moment is to excuse myself from the situation and go somewhere quiet. There I am able to take a breath and refocus, then I can remember to do at least one, or all of these three things.

Choose Calm and Communicate - With yourself or someone else.
Action - Do something that will change your circumstance for the better.
Release - Authentically let go of what no longer serves you … forgive.
Solutions - Focus full attention on your best solution. Get/Allow Support.

This is all a process. It can take awhile to make it a new conscious habit. Be patient and compassionate with yourself and others. For now, let's take a look at each of these items in more detail.

CHOOSE CALM AND COMMUNICATE

Calm is always a choice, not always the easy thing to do, but it serves us well. When we choose calm we are able to think more clearly and focus on the solutions that will help us out in the moment.

There are many methods to choosing calm, one of my favorites is simply to start focusing on the breath. It's your body's natural way of relaxing. As you breathe in you claim calm for yourself, with each breath out you let go of what no longer serves you. You can also count yourself down as you're breathing as well. With each number, you let your mind and body relax more and more. I have a short meditation on my website that is helpful to bring back your ability to choose calm as well.

Remember, it's within your power to choose how to react to anything that comes your way. Your perception is a ruler to where you will be going, and you can learn to perceive things in a way that is supportive of what you want. This is one of the ways to continually choose to own your power. The more you own your calm, the easier is gets. It's like building muscle, and you get stronger at it each time. Try it out, be committed to the process and notice how much your life gets better each and every time.

Now, for **Communication**, sometimes it's our self that we need to communicate with, and sometimes it is someone else. If it's you, then you will be using the Fear Into Power tool, it's further along in this book. This is the tool that will help you recognize your unconscious thinking and assist you in retraining your brain in an deliberate way.

If it's someone else that has you in a spin, then you will want to have some constructive and effective communication with them. Again, a tool called Constructive Communication, that is coming up here in your book.

In all my years of working with people, I would say that 95% of the problems that we face with relationships are because of a lack of good communication. When you own your ability to voice your concerns, desires, frustrations, etc. in a way that is empowering, it changes everything! If you want to take a peek at the chapter on communication now, you are more than welcome.

ACTION

As you find yourself starting to go down the hill to hell, it can be really hard to know what kind of action to take. Chances are, you aren't thinking clearly and your probably wrapped up in the drama or trauma of whatever is taking place.

That's why it good to know ahead of time what you would do in those situations. We can program into our awareness an alternate route to take, that way we can put ourselves on a bit of auto drive while figuring things out.

The task at hand then would be for you to take a few minutes and determine for yourself what those triggers are for you. It could be difficult people, or situations you know you'll be in, basically, anything that may be anxiety, stress, anger, or worry producing.

Here's another exercise for you to do, write down a list of at least 5 options that you can take to be able to choose calm next time you're having a "moment".

It could be as easy as taking a "time out" in the restroom, slowly count to five, and own the ability to choose calm. For those moments, call someone that makes sense to you to help work it out constructively, who will help with positive solutions. Maybe listen to a quick calming meditation, podcast, or book. Focus on calm music. Walk in nature.

Be creative, picture yourself doing this while you're writing it down, feel the feeling of calm now. When you find yourself in a possible moment in the future, you just programmed in a new route!

When we do this, we retrain the brain. We start to re-pattern and create a new mental roadway for dealing with the hard moments in life.

RELEASE/LET GO

Sometimes it's just not worth it to feel so bad about something. There are those moments when you can weigh things out and make a decision to just let it go.

It's always a good idea to let go of things, experiences, and people that cause you to go down that hill to hell as much as possible. Make a commitment to yourself to be aware and willing to make the changes for your good to happen.

Pay attention, how much of the time are you going down the hill for someone else … it's not even your issue! I've had so many people tell me that they've been so upset at other peoples problems that they can't change, and the person who has the problem doesn't do anything about it. That's just madness. Support your friend by focusing on the possible solutions that may be available for them.

Think back to how many times you've gone there … been furious or anxious, and wished you hadn't. Did that result with you feeling guilt, remorse or shame?

How many times would you have been better off if you'd just been calm and communicated with yourself and let it go? Better yet, what did you ever gain in the long run by letting your anger or anxiety get the best of you?

Releasing our hold on being right in situations is very challenging. Much of the time our unconscious mind says that we need to be right, we desire to be heard, and we want what we want. We go into fight/flight mode and if we just push enough it will certainly happen, but at what cost? Letting go can be the most powerful thing to do. It may not look like it in the moment, but, for those on an empowered path, you stay sane and find a better approach to the issues. This is yet another way that you can choose to own your power!

SOLUTIONS

It's a fact that many of us have been trained to place our focus on the problems of life. Take a minute and think about the conversations that you've had over the last few days. How much of the time was the topic on the bad things that were happening, someone did something to someone, this person is doing something to ruin their life or someone else's. When you watch the news, much of the focus is on the messed up world we are in, not on all the solutions that are happening or the new inventions to fix the problems.

Interestingly enough, according to the National Science Foundation, our subconscious brain is thinking from the negative about 80% of the day … every day! Incredibly, 95% of our challenging thoughts are repetitive! We are rather programmed to be this way, the good news is that we now have the information to reprogram how we are thinking and be able to focus on the solutions to the challenges that we all face.

Each time you stop the car at the top of the hill and take the steps to move through the struggles of life you are creating a new path in your brain. You are creating new habits to function through the hard times with grace. You're owning your ability to choose the destination that will keep you at the top of the hill longer and longer … and when you go down the hill to hell again, you won't stay there as long!

SUPPORT

Lean in to those who are geared toward your best and highest happening. Allow!
Everyone needs a lift sometime.

Find Support, whether it be family, friends, associates, therapists, spiritual practitioners, AA or any other person/organization that is of service to the community. I've found that the clients with the most challenges are those that tend to isolate. Unfortunately this doesn't do well for the mind and feelings that need a new direction. It's like we have driven our car into a cave and it's dark and we are unable to find the exit. Allow for support from others who know how to direct you out of the darkness.

Also allow support from the Universal Intelligence, God or whatever you know your higher power as. This is the greatest support, lean in to your connection to source … more about this coming up.

Now that you have stopped your car, your mind, from the deep slide into the break down and you've gotten yourself somewhat calm, it's time to move up the Gameboard. Your TOOL BOX is ahead! In the Tools you will find the "Do This" action steps that will assist you in creating a conscious awareness of what you choose to do in all areas of life.

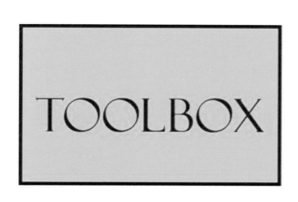

TOOLS FOR TRANSFORMATION

Intention
Mindfulness
Fear Into Power
Positive Pondering
Power Statements
Choice Point Timeline
Constructive Communication
Victimization Loop
Meditation
Visioning
Purposeful Prayer

THE TOOLS

This is the part of the game where you are in process, becoming Aware that you are Aware, and you learn to use new innovative and transformational tools. Somewhat like the actual tools that you would find in your toolbox, these are your means to get the job done.

These tools are the practice that will help you create a more conscious awareness, new intentional beliefs, and constructive habits. The next section of this book is all about the Tools, in the car analogy, this would be the Car Owner's Manual of Directions.

Much of the time it takes about three weeks to change a habit. Once you do make the adjustment, it will be fixed into your course. You will have created an Unconsciously Conscious Mindset and then you will move to the top of the board to CRUISE CONTROL.

"Imagine a cork, floating on a body of water, as being your connected point of view. That is when you are soaring, that's where your appreciation is high. You are tuned in, tapped in, turned on. You are up there in that high natural frequency. Now take hold of the cork and hold it under the water. That is what negative emotion is. That's where you are ornery, irritated, insecure, fitful, frustrated, overwhelmed, blameful, or guilty. That's the negative emotion. The good news is, in the moment that you take your attention away from whatever it is that's holding you in that vibration, you let go of the cork and it floats right back to the top. And that is perhaps the most important thing that we want you to hear from us today. It is natural for your cork to float. It is natural for you to feel good. That is what is natural. Anything less than that is not natural." ~Abraham/Hicks

Being in Cruise Control is the constant goal, this is the place that we want to live in as much as possible. To be in cruise contol in your day to day life, you're in the flow. You are making choices that are life affirming and that lead you in the direction of your intentions and you're having a good time while on the road. You have passengers in your car that are supportive and loving, and you navigate around the other drivers that aren't in alignment with your conscious drive.

In cruise control you have taken the unconscious negative thoughts and re-routed them to be a strong conscious intention.

If you imagine the road of your life it could look something like this ...

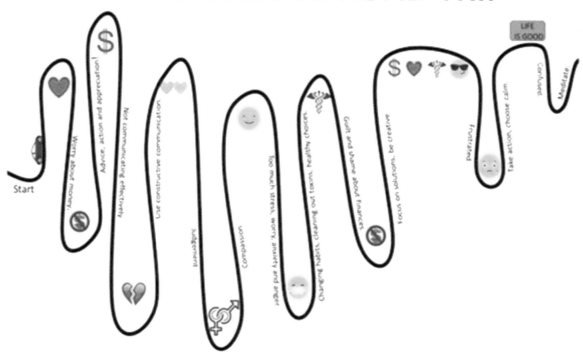

DO THIS TO MOVE UP THE BOARD FASTER

THIS IS A PROCESS … BE PATIENT WITH YOURSELF. Not exactly easy, though it is simple to do. You may find that you nail the current challenge in one great moment, and it is a done deal! You have let go of or transformed that "thing" and life is good. Or you are in re-direction, and you are taking a new route that leads you to a better place than where you were. Sometimes you are not going to get it exactly the way you want it the first time. The trick is that you have made your life better and there are open possibilities to make it even better.

It is all about moving forward. Each time you practice these tools, you will create a new habit, and a new "normal" that brings you more happiness.

Keep these things in mind as you drive on.

- This is a practice that is developed over time.
- It's extremely helpful to find something, anything, to appreciate daily.
- If you falter, get back up again. Realign yourself. Find someone that you can trust who is a mentor, teacher, and guide that you can meet with on a weekly basis. A therapist, minister, sponsor, etc.
- Challenge your perspective, be open to new ideas.
- Slow down and create a natural rhythm.

- Remember what is good in the world and keep driving toward that feeling of happiness, contentment, and calm.
- Use this present moment as an opportunity to overcome fears. BE BRAVE.
- Nature is a healing force, use that energy and focus deep attention on nurturing the mind, body, psyche/soul.
- Appreciate family and friends, love them madly and deeply! IT FEELS GOOD!
- Have days where there is no agenda at all. Create the freedom to do what you want, when you want, and make it OK.
- When you are at the bottom, help someone who is worse off.
- Let the past go and forgive your unconscious behavior.
- Make a change in lifestyle, nutrition, and get more exercise.
- Keep learning! There are resources in the back of this book for some of my favorite teachers/ mentors.
- Commit to using the tools daily, go the extra mile.
- Constantly challenge yourself.
- Focus on winning your game daily.
- Be present with all the twists and turns the process will take.
- Navigate the currents somewhat like navigating the freeways.
- Be In The Flow
- Watch for road signs along the way.
- Dump Your Trauma Trunk.
- Allow the Universal Intelligence to be your Co-Pilot
- Do This! No trying allowed!

Kudos for all your effort, commitment and time spent on you!

THE NAVIGATIONAL SYSTEM

You are always in a choice point ... every minute of every day. In that choice moment you get to determine how you will perceive your life within your circumstances and what actions you will take. Many people have talked about the "fork in the road," and if they had only gone in the other direction their life would have been so different... and most times they believe it would have been better. One of my main intentions in writing this book was to help people understand how they make those choices, and more importantly how to make the choice of choosing the road best traveled.

Everything can be taken from a man but one thing: the last of human freedoms - to choose one's attitude in any given set of circumstances, to choose one's own way. ~Viktor E. Frankl

These three words will determine your experience.

Intention sets the roadmap to where you are going.
      Attention keeps the focus on the desired destination.
            Perception will keep you on your deliberate path.

INTENTION

"There is one quality which one must possess to win, and that is definiteness of purpose, the knowledge of what one wants, and a burning desire to possess it." ~Napoleon Hill

We talked about intention at the description for the START point of the board game, and you have had a little time since reading that to get a stronger idea of what your intentions are. You may have also noticed

25

that since reading and writing your intentions in the intention exercise that you have a trouble with holding fast and making those intentions happen. It might be worth the moment to look back at that chapter and revisit the exercise, this can be where the great shifts happen for you. Notice if any of your intentions cause you to feel like It might not be attainable for you. Why? Take note of these things, they will be worked through as you go further.

For now, it is a good idea to get that intention definitely set. Here are a few tips:

- ✓ Get a picture of it in your mind. A *Vision Board works well, helps with visioning, and maps it in the conscious mind.
- ✓ Daydream and imagine that there are no limitations to the best outcome. Be open to inspiration, allow your creativity to flow. The highest part of you already knows the best outcome for the best to happen. Catch that greater vision. Make it like you are the director of the movie of your new life.
- ✓ FEEL what it would be like to have it now. Allow the feeling of joy, own the confidence, deep gratitude for the ability to create this dream and turn it into a new reality. Enthusiasm, if you can muster some, is always a good vibration that the Universe hears well.
- ✓ Intention is the course of action that you intend to follow and the purpose that guides your actions.
- ✓ Be clear, focused, determined and 100% committed, then take the actions to make those dreams, wants, desires, and purpose happen.

Create and write down what you would like to achieve for these areas of your life to the best of your ability in this moment. Many times, I have asked my clients this question and they look me in with pure honesty and say that they have no idea what they want. At all! So, I look at them and give one little suggestion… would you like to be happier? Every single time they have said yes. If you're not in a place to make a lot of intentions, just make one or two simple ones that you can keep your attention on. Another example of a simple, effective intention is to be calmer.

Important when setting an intention, this is the new route in your mind, and it has to go from your mind into action. If we have the intention and it's swirling around the mind with no direction, it just stays in the mind. When you put action into the mix it takes it out of the mind and into creation (it's happening).

Bottom line, you must begin taking actions that match your intention. Example for this is when you decide to be a bit happier, you create a list of actions for that happy to happen. It could look like; I'm watching only funny, lighthearted TV and movies, I am only listening to uplifting music, I'm enjoying time in nature, I'm hanging out with festive friends, etc. These are your new roads to travel in your mind, and then your road of life.

ATTENTION

All day … every day … ask yourself this especially important question.

"Where is my attention?" Is my attention on the problem, the drama, old unresolved business? Is any of it attached to your INTENTION?

Putting your attention on your intention on a regular basis is life changing. It is so important, the more you actually start paying more attention to the little voice in your head, the more you'll notice that what it's saying isn't supportive of a great experience.

To play this game at your best, be aware of where your attention is … all the time. Where your attention is, you go. So, in a big way your attention is driving your car most of the time … and, the attention is programmed, so it will keep going around and around to all the same kinds of drama, trauma, and problems. It really can seem like you are a victim to life's circumstances! Notice how you may tend to focus on negative crap. No judgement about this, now you have an opportunity to turn that around and focus your full attention on any solutions. What do you really want? How do you make your best and highest happen? Listen to that voice in your head. It lets you know the focus of your attention, and now you can change it.

It is always all right to have problems, we're all human. It is part of life. Stop judging where you or someone else is at … it does nothing for you. We all got an imperfect program that we have been running. The great news is that now we get to pay attention and be awake while at the wheel of our beautifully empowered car.

PERCEPTION

"Your perspective is always limited by how much you know. Expand your knowledge and you will transform your mind."

"Life has everything in it, but you only see what your perception allows you to see." ~Dr. Bruce Lipton

The environment, the way that you were brought up, and your own ideas/beliefs have developed the way that you view yourself, and the way that you perceive the world around you. The perception that you have of let's just say, *everything*, is what determines what you will do with the situations that come up in your life.

Your view of your own self-worth, your relationships, your job, your appearance, and your place in the world will all determine your position. If you are unhappy, unhealthy, unsuccessful, or feeling unloved, it may be that you need a shift in your perception.

Lucky for you, that is a lot of what you will be changing for yourself! Keep reading!

"We can control our lives by controlling our perceptions." ~Bruce H. Lipton

It just comes back to the saying, "You just don't know what you don't know." The best thing to do is to come from what you can know, and you can know a new truth for yourself. It is as simple as that. Owning your ability to come from a clear perception is one of the greatest gifts that you can ever give yourself. Truly!

So, let's look more at what your perception has to do with how you are getting around that gameboard.

I showed this picture to a client, and they thought it was a bad idea. For this person, they had way too much. Too much material stuff, drugs/alcohol, responsibility, and too much stress. They looked at this picture and the perspective was that this would just bring on bigger problems.

All the other people that I showed the photo to thought that the fish moving to a larger bowl was a great idea. What did you think? If it gave you a more positive feeling, use this as a visualization for moving up your board. Imagine if you were like that fish and moving into a new experience. Own the feeling of new freedom.

In the way that I grew up my perception of myself was not great. I did not feel worthy, valuable, or lovable. When you get told that you are cute but not that smart as a foundation, it would appear that many things can go downhill from there. What happens when you stop being cute? As a kid I developed severely bucked teeth, and I was chubby, maybe a little bit more than just chubby. At times, I was a brat, I really acted up in class for a few years, one year I was sent to the principal's office three times. It was really not an accident that I did not have a lot of friends. I did not realize it at the time because I was just in it, at the time it was just what I knew of life. I had incredibly low self-esteem. With this lack of worth, thoughts of being stupid, feeling awkward, poor, and unattractive, I created many embarrassing and sad moments.

It has taken me many, many years to come to the perception of my life as I know it. I spend lots of time in introspection and working through the beliefs one by one to come to the truth of who I choose to be. I still continue getting rid of judgement and I use compassion to come to the right mindset that holds the roadmap to my future.

How about you? I think we can all relate to having at least one crazy *** moment. Are you holding any judgement of yourself? Do you have judgement of others? How is that perception working for you?

For many of us the perceptions that we have around our body and the bodies of others is one of the most distorted. We have been shown photos of the "perfect" body since we were all young, and unconsciously most of us will never measure up to that image. So, we own a perspective of who we are physically that is not realistic and can be extremely painful and destructive. Begin the process of changing your perception of your beautiful body, nurture and be kind to the vehicle that makes your experience possible.

Your perception of everything creates how you proceed around the board.

MIND ROAD TRIP FOR PERSPECTIVE

Think of the following words and ponder what you think of them.

Write down your first thoughts to each. Do not judge, be open to what comes to the surface of your mind. Ask yourself specific questions at this point. Be honest and know that as you move further with this book, the answers might possibly change. Examples of specific questions with regard to money are what does money mean for me, how does money make me feel, when did I first feel anything around money, who gave me an example of how to be with money and why do I care?

Money	God	Politics
Health	War	Drugs
Peace	Success	Husband
Men	Alcohol	Wife
Women	Religion	Kids
Love	Stress	

Are those first thoughts supportive of what your intention is?

Here's an example: Money.

> Money is dirty.
> Money is the root of all evil.
> Money doesn't come to me.
> I cannot keep money.
> Money equals stress.
> Is this supportive of someone who wants a lot of cash?

It will probably surprise you how many thoughts are unintentionally causing you to have exactly what you do not want.

Another example: Men/Women
Men/Women are unfaithful, liars, cheats.
They will hurt me (emotionally, mentally, or physically)
They will let me down.
I will not get to do what I want if I have a partner.
I must have a rich man.
I must have a beautiful woman.

Your perception shows up in how loving, happy, and balanced your relationships are. Believe it or not, your perceptions also affect the health of your body, the abundance/success in your life and how happy you are.

If you are having challenges in the areas of your life, look at how your perception is. Time to make the adjustments … TOOLS AHEAD!

THE TOOLS FOR TRANSFORMATION

New Rules, Innovative Tools and Clever Hacks for the Conscious Journey to Your Destination.

Be Mindful
Fear Into Power
Power Statements
Choice Point Timeline
Constructive Communication
Victimization Loop
Mindful Meditation
Creative Visioning
Power Packed Prayer
Daily Alignment and Balance

BE MINDFUL

AVOID ACCIDENTAL THINKING

Sometimes when you are getting to the answer of anything you can look at the opposite and it can help to define it better. The opposite of Mindful would be Mindless, and as you can see from the amount of accidental driving that we have on our actual roads, there's a lot of mindless drivers creating a lot of damage. So, how are they actually mindless and in accidental thinking? They usually aren't paying attention to the road, sometimes they have missed the exit and are trying to get back in and they cause an accident, they may be driving too close to other drivers, or maybe they are under an influence and not totally present. You can see how being mindless create chaos.

Mindful being the opposite creates calm. Mindful equals attention on the road, paying attention to road signs along the way, mindful is giving space and holding healthy boundaries, mindful is being present and working *through* addictions.

Another part of being Mindful is to have a better understanding of how the mind/brain actually works, and more importantly to use that information to reroute destructive habits, beliefs and ideas. I would say that this version of Mindful is about being curious and open to new ideas and beliefs. It's being able to look at all things with logical, reasonable, and deductive thinking. There will be more on this very soon… keep driving.

If you want to go around the track fully charged and powerful, then becoming more in the present moment, being aware and intentional is vital. #1 in the Tools for Transformation is to recognize the unconscious/unaware thinking you have going on.

Your thoughts are tremendously powerful. Think for a minute about your life currently. Notice how you manifested things around you. You thought; I will do this as my job, or maybe I will accept that job as mine because I want the money I will earn. You may have thought, I will pursue that man/woman and create a partner, a love of my life, or you let yourself be picked and settled for who picked you. One of my favorites, you went about the business of intentionally creating children, or maybe not so intentionally.

When you are not focused and intentional, your mind chatter is instinctive and mostly unconscious. As science will testify, our negative thinking is most of the time in fear mode with our attention on the negative aspects of life. My friends, this is the kind of thinking that creates roadblocks, detours, and accidents.

When I am working with clients, it's my job to notice within the conversation, the thoughts, beliefs, and ideas that they are creating their life from. This is the point of their unconscious creation, that part of them that does not know what they don't know. Using that information, then I am able to point out to them how they are creating what they don't want. There are so many examples of how this shows up in every aspect of our lives, and some examples I have heard are …

- *I try so hard and do not get what I want.*
- *I am so worried all the time.*
- *I am broken.*
- *All the good guys/girls are taken.*
- *I am not smart.*
- *I am not strong enough.*

I will probably say this a million times more in my lifetime … life really is an out picturing of our conscious or unconscious thinking. Basically, you are either in conscious planning and construction mode, or you're in the unconscious improvising and destruction mode. The Universe does not care what mode you're in, the Intelligence that is creating all things is responding to your thinking and your feelings.

Our brain uses information to process what that thinking is.

We perceive something, some situation, what someone has said or done, and we come up with a thought about it. Could be a constructive or destructive thought … your choice. One key to life is to make sure that you know that you do have a choice.

So, how do you own that choice?

You can choose to pay attention to the mind chatter, and with that statement you might ask, "what is mind chatter." One of my favorite authors, Michael Singer, really has a great conversation about that special subject. *"There is nothing more important to true growth than realizing that you are not the voice of the mind — you are the one who hears it."* ~Michael A. Singer, *The Untethered Soul*. I highly recommend this book. Great for understanding our inner voice more deeply.

Many people may get triggered by the idea that they have a little voice in their head. In fact, I have worked with many clients who quite literally had a little voice in their head that they knew was not their own. It's a very disturbing situation, and fortunately all the people that came to me with that particular problem are resolved with the voice, and they in the process came to own their own voice more powerfully.

With what we are doing with the whole car analogy, let's consider the voice in your head the #2 Driver in the backseat. Otherwise known as the kid in the backseat. You can even give them a name, mine is Audi in the backseat. She can get really chatty sometimes. What is that little voice of your kid in the backseat of your mind thinking and saying to you? It's a good idea to listen to them, in many ways they have been the primary driver and causing the chaos.

I've had some very amusing moments with clients about their kid in the backseat. I have described to many clients that they so do not want to listen to their inner child that it's like they are driving a limousine, and they have rolled up the window between them and the backseat! Then, looking back and saying I can't hear you, really, you need to be quiet! Some of the names that they have given to the kid are amusing as well.

For you, come up with something that you feel comfortable with, a name or phrase that you can use for them that brings them emotionally closer to you. Imagine looking back over the seat and having a "conversation" with that younger version of you. A conversation where they know that you, the #2 Adult driver is listening.

Examples of this are when you have anxiety, and you stop the car. This part of communication is listening to what the anxiety is about. You as the adult are listening to the younger you say something like, I'm anxious that this will happen, like it happened before, I'm worried that they won't like me, they didn't like me in the past, etc.

Here is another quote from the fabulous Mr. Singer, he's saying it well, "You are not your thoughts; you are aware of your thoughts. You are not your emotions; you feel emotions. You are not your body; you look at it in the mirror and experience this world through its eyes and ears. You are the conscious being who is aware that you are aware of all these inner and outer things." ~Michael Singer, *The Untethered Soul*.

MIND ROAD TRIP FOR MIND/BRAIN CHATTER

For the next few days just pay attention to your own little voice in your head. Write down what it is saying. No judgement! Just notice for now. Notice especially when you have feelings of anger, worry, anxiety, or stress, that is where those unconscious negative thoughts can be easily found. Be patient with yourself if you find that there are a lot of challenging beliefs and ideas that you have been holding about yourself or others. You are in process, and you get to change these ideas soon!

"Your thoughts are incredibly powerful. Choose yours wisely."
~ Joe Dispenza, You Are the Placebo: Making Your Mind Matter

MIND BRAIN CHATTER

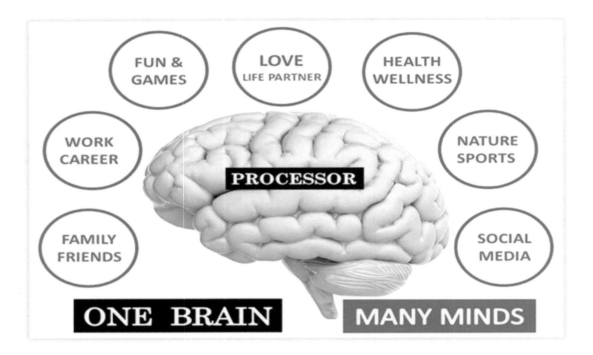

I have been talking professionally with people for my entire life, and one thing that I know from all those thousands of conversations is that people have a lot of "chatter" going on in their heads. When I used to be a Hair Designer, I spent most of my time listening to my clients and asking the why, what, where, when, and how questions. I enjoyed hearing other people's stories and I have the ability to envision what they said in my mind, many times they would be surprised at how much I remembered when they would see me again. I was not a therapist at that time, so I didn't question the "chatter" that they would share. That doesn't mean that I didn't notice and question in my own mind how challenging it would be to have such an extensive and emotional conversation about things that are not important in the day-to-day business of life. One example of this kind of chatter is when you go over and over again on what you would have said to someone that you may be angry with without taking some form of action to make it better. I have witnessed many client cases, (and in my own life) where a client will come in and share with me the chatter that has been going round and round in their mind. Many times, it's that they are angry with someone. They have been mulling over and over what the person did/said… for days, even weeks, sometimes years. Not only has this taken up headspace, but it's also creating energetic tension in the body and with the other person. My job is to show them, and now you, a new perspective of the chatter and give them the tools to re-write the new scenario of what is wanted/intended for things to be.

Chatter simply doesn't matter. Chatter in my definition is the mind rolling around in thoughts that are not constructive, productive, uplifting, motivating or affirmative. Chatter is letting the kid in the back seat go on and on without checking them. You can tell when the chatter is rolling when you feel like you're in the Victimization Loop. More about this tool coming up.

Let's look at some more information about your mind/brain, that miraculous organ in your head that is directing you in the traffic of life.

- Your mind controls your information and energy.
- Your mind is co-creating the wonderful or terrible experiences in life.
- Every new thought creates a unique pattern of your brain roadmaps.
- You have a natural ability to restructure your brain and your thinking process.
- Your mind is always busy designing the very structure of your brain that helps you make decisions.
- The brain will picture what to create based on where your attention and perception is. Think about it like this, your brain is "thinking" in pictures. When we say, "Don't run" or "Stop chewing with your mouth open" to a child, their mind is picturing running and chewing with an open mouth. When *you* say anything with don't, won't, can't, etc., the brain is picturing whatever follows. Be aware and say and focus on what you want.
- The brain works with the body to produce the chemistry we need for self-healing.
- The brain is tuning in and acquiring inspired information … intelligence. Your intelligence is not in the little brain, it's like you are picking up on Satellite and using a guidance system to help with Navigation.
- Your brain is always transmitting with your heart, and your heart is always connecting to your brain. This process this programming into your unique navigational system each and every day. It is a big part of determining your road map destination.

"If the brain expects that a treatment will work, it sends healing chemicals into the bloodstream, which facilitates that. That is why the placebo effect is so powerful for every type of healing. And the opposite is equally true and equally powerful: When the brain expects that a therapy will not work, it doesn't. It's called the "nocebo" effect." ~ Bruce H. Lipton

THE MIND IN ACTION

Another way of looking at the neural network in the brain is to think of this as the roads of your mind. You have regular patterns, better known as habits, that you follow. This is your "current operating system." Don't think of it as right or wrong, bad, or good, it just is how you have gone about your life up to this point. When you consider those parts of your life that you want to change, this is the starting point. Just as much as you say, "This is who I am," or "It's how I've always done it," this is an opportunity to pave a new road in your mind that is in alignment with what you really want. Being stuck, unhappy, resentful, bitter, or depressed isn't who you are, it's just where you've been.

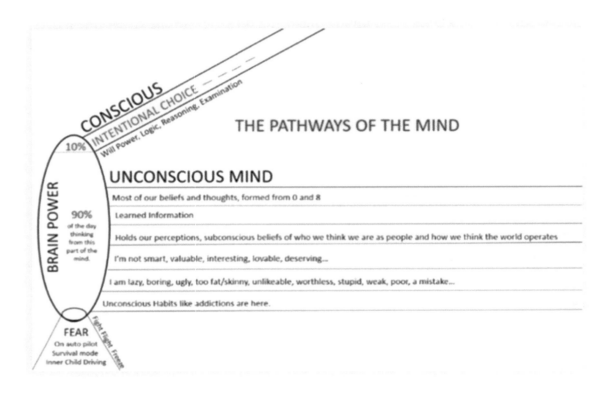

Transforming the mind is so much easier when you have a better understanding of what the mind does and how it does it. To be clear, you have one brain, and many minds. When you begin each new moment there is a unique part of your mind/brain that you are accessing that is involved in doing the actions, speaking your words, individual mannerism, basically all the business of your day-to-day activities. Think about it, who are you when you're with friends, work associates, your partner, your kids, and your parents. The many minds that make up you!

"Mind is the brain in action." ~Joe Dispenza, Becoming Superhuman

Think about your day … what is your normal?

At home, do you start with a cup of coffee/tea? Do you tune into social media or the news? Do you go to the gym? Do you meditate first thing? Do you call someone? What are the automatic actions you don't even think about and just do?

How about at your job, are you at work the same time every day? What are the repetitive thoughts that you may have at work? What are your habits there?

Do you have a nightly routine? Many people have regular shows that they like to watch to "unwind." Do you have any drinks or other substances to chill out at the end of a long day? How about comfort food that is comforting? Our minds can certainly be on an auto pilot with that, many people shared with me that they have gone to the refrigerator and are sitting eating without even realizing that they got up to get the food. Totally unconscious behavior, in this instance the kid in the backseat put up the window in the limousine and told the adult, "No worries, I got this! We're just going to enjoy this moment and nothing else matters." That's all fine and good until the adult realizes that they are now suffering whatever consequences from that behavior.

We do have all these ways that we "Be," and many people have said to me that, "it's just who I am." We get so stuck in the habitual thoughts that we just think this is just what I do, it's our lot in life. Well, it is until it isn't.

To really understand our ability to get stuck in one lane highway in your mind I'm going to give you an example of someone very close to me, my Mother, who is now deceased. She had a time in her 40's to 50's where she massively got stuck in a routine that felt safe for her and she became Agoraphobic, she had extreme anxiety and panic attacks when she left the protection of her home. This lasted for ten years until finally she had enough, the safety had become jail. One day she changed her routine and went for a walk down the block, the next day around the block, then around the neighborhood, until finally she got in the car and experienced the world in a new way. I was so impressed with her, she did not go to a therapist, she just made a commitment to herself and went with it. She did a similar thing with ending the habit of smoking, she smoked cigarettes from 13 years old until New Year's day during her 60th year she decided that she had enough with that addiction and quit cold turkey with no outside help. This mindless, unconscious habit was replaced by a mindful, conscious intention to no longer be a slave to the programed mind. She rewrote the program and so can you.

Here's how you do it… Consciously pay attention to your day and to what your attention has been on. This is just to begin the process of understanding more of how your mind works. To be clear, your mind gets set in borders that you have created for yourself. Be willing to step out of your, "regular daily routine" and mix things up a bit. Like my mother, she walked until she got in her car, then she owned the driver's seat and made life happen.

One way to create a new mental program is through imagination, when you imagine you create a new approach in your mind. To do this you want to think outside of your own box, the Mental Road Trip will help you with that. Get comfortable and take some time for this exercise.

MIND ROAD TRIP FOR EXPANSION

Imagine in your mind that you have been driving the roads of your childhood neighborhood all your life up to now, you never left. It is comfortable, safe, and predictable.

Now imagine that you are going on your first fabulous road trip. What is your intention for this trip? What areas of your life are getting an upgrade?

Think about how exciting it is to see new things, experience great new adventures, this mind trip is exciting, fun, a wildly sane and safe adventure.

Picture in your mind where you are directing yourself to go. Let your imagination go free, unlimited, and expansive. Keep focused on the feelings that are in line with your intention, feel the feelings that lift you up.

Once you have that image of your best and highest for now, take a mental snapshot of the image. Hold that in the forefront of your mind and write down on paper how that feels for you, and some actions that you can take to make it happen. Can be small actions like my mother walking down the block, or as big as you feel comfortable with.

After you have done the previous exercise for a few days, switch to this exercise.

Take your phone and set a reminder for first thing tomorrow morning. The reminder is to let you know that today is brand new day. *I get to choose*! Then do things differently, it can be something subtle like choosing different kinds of clothes to wear that day. Maybe if you pick up your phone first thing you wait till after breakfast. If you turn on the news first thing, maybe switch to an inspiring podcast. Might be that you shower first then have that first cup o' joe. Maybe get up and take a walk first thing to get the blood moving. You decide … just pick something each day to switch in your routine.

Another option for this exercise is to use a physical calendar and you could put some new habits to eliminate or create. Small changes add up. Many of my clients who do this have looked back at their calendar and it gives a new perspective for how much they have positively changed.

SUBCONSCIOUS DESTRUCTIVE THINKING

Let's get even more clear, when I said earlier that most of our thoughts are subconscious and negative, I was not kidding. For most of us we are driving a course that is being navigated by the programming that we have taken on during our lifetime. All the people that have influenced you have drawn the map that you are travelling on. This is your opportunity to recognize the program and make the necessary adjustments.

I love this quote from Abraham and Ester Hicks …

"I Have Complete Control Over My Own Thoughts … You can find yourself in an endless loop where you explain that you feel negative because of the negative behavior of someone else. But if, instead, you take control of your own emotions and you think an improved thought because it feels better to do so, you will discover that no matter how the negative trend got started, you can turn it around. You have no real control of what anyone else is doing with their Vibration (or with their actions, for that matter), but you have complete control over your own thoughts, Vibrations, emotions, and point of attraction."

Some examples of Subconscious Destructive Thinking are …

This always happens and I never get what I want! Coming to an overall conclusion based on a single event or one piece of evidence. If something bad happens once, you expect it to happen again and again. Such thoughts often include the words "always" and "never."
I forgot to finish that project on time. I never manage to do things right.
He did not want to go out with me. I will always be lonely.

I am sifting and sorting to the worst view: Concentrating on the negatives while ignoring the positives; ignoring important information that contradicts your (negative) view of the situation.
I know my boss said most of my work was great, but he also said there were a number of mistakes that had to be corrected … he must think I am really hopeless!

It is all or nothing: Thinking in black and white terms (e.g., things are right or wrong, good, or bad). It is a tendency to view things at the extremes with no middle ground.
I made so many mistakes … If I cannot do it perfectly, I might as well not bother.
I will not be able to get all of this done, so I may as well not start it.
This job is so bad … there is nothing good about it at all.

It is all my fault: Taking responsibility for something that is not your error. Thinking that what people say or do is a reaction to you or is in some way related to you.
Johns in a terrible mood. It must have been something I did.
It is obvious she doesn't like me, otherwise she would've said hello.
I did not get the job because of how I look …

The worst things always happen! Overestimating the chances of disaster, expecting something unbearable or intolerable to happen. Such thoughts often begin with "What if …?"
I'm going to make a fool of myself, and people will laugh at me.
What if I have not turned the iron off and the house burns down?

If I feel like this, it must be true. Mistaking feelings for facts. Negative things you feel about yourself are held to be true because they feel true.
I feel like a failure; and so, I am a failure.
I feel ugly, so, I must be ugly.
I feel hopeless; therefore, my situation must be hopeless.

I know what you are thinking. Making assumptions about other people's thoughts, feelings, and behaviors without checking the evidence.
John's talking to Molly, so he likes her more than me.
I can tell he hates my shirt.
I could tell he thought I was stupid in the interview.

I am sure I know what's going to happen … it always does. Anticipating an outcome and assuming your prediction is an established fact. These negative expectations can be self- fulfilling: predicting what we would do on the basis of past behavior may prevent the possibility of change.

I have always been like this; I'll never be able to change.

It is not going to work out so there's not much point even trying.

This relationship is sure to fail.

I shoulda, coulda or woulda … we must do better! Using "should," "ought," or "must" statements can set up unrealistic expectations of yourself and others. It involves operating by rigid rules and not allowing for flexibility.

I should not get angry.

People should be nice to me all the time.

I should be able to kick this habit.

All the good does not make up for the bad. A tendency to exaggerate the importance of negative information or experiences, while trivializing or reducing the significance of positive information or experiences.

She said she does want me in the class, but she did not ask me … she probably is just saying that she wants me to be nice.

Supporting my friend when her mother died still does not make up for that time, I got angry at her last year. I am not a good friend.

Think about the subconscious negative thoughts in your life.

Write down some of the phrases, sentences, of the messages you have been given or heard that create difficulty for you. Right now, it is just a moment to begin the recognition of what you've been thinking. Remember, no judgement!

FREE YOUR MIND AND THE BEST WILL FOLLOW

Are you curious on how you came to be thinking all those unconscious thoughts? You did not come out of your mother's womb that way, it was all learned.

From when you were still in the womb, you were absorbing how to manage your emotions from your mother. Then when you came into the world, your parents, siblings, teachers, and other influences gave you direction, definition and showed you how to drive your unique and beautiful car.

You were in the backseat of your parents/caregiver's car between the ages of 0 and 8 and you took on the program of what they knew to teach and show you. Think about how many things you do that are just like one or both of your parents. We learn what love looks like, how to talk with each other, how to manage money, we also learn what character and integrity looks like. Another interesting observation, if you have older siblings, they can be another influence in the way that your mind was formed.

Here is another way to think about this … think about your computer or your cell phone. When it was first made at the manufacturer there was not much to it, just the possibility of what it has to offer. Then they put in the programs that gives the device the ability to do the many different things that we expect from them on a daily basis. Internet, social media, photos, apps for this and that. They all had to be downloaded into the hard drive. Most of us do not even think about it; we just know that they are there, and we use these programs without even thinking about it. Our brain is like an operating system. We have programs that determine our identity, worth, success, what kind of partner we desire, what kind of partner we will be, etc.

MIND OVER MATTER

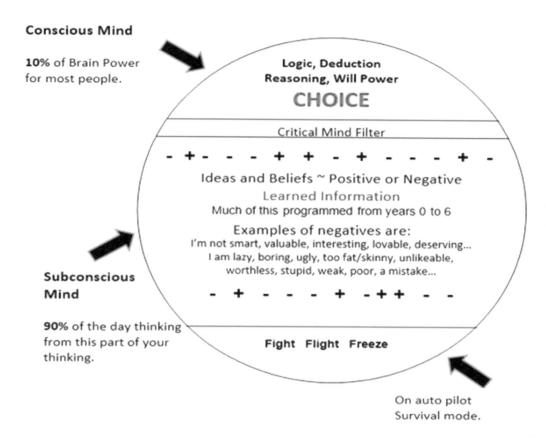

Conscious Mind

10% of Brain Power for most people.

Logic, Deduction
Reasoning, Will Power
CHOICE

Critical Mind Filter

- + - - + + - + - - - + -

Ideas and Beliefs ~ Positive or Negative
Learned Information
Much of this programmed from years 0 to 6
Examples of negatives are:
I'm not smart, valuable, interesting, lovable, deserving...
I am lazy, boring, ugly, too fat/skinny, unlikeable,
worthless, stupid, weak, poor, a mistake...

- + - - - + - + + - -

Subconscious Mind

90% of the day thinking from this part of your thinking.

Fight Flight Freeze

On auto pilot
Survival mode.

Take a moment and look at the diagram of Mind Over Matter.
This represents your thinking and how we took on our "program."
Imagine that this is your mind, notice that there are four definite parts to the power of your thinking.

At the bottom of the chart there is the primitive area of your mind. That is when you are not consciously thinking at all, you are in auto pilot. When you you're your primitive mind more structured it is working for you to fight, maybe to flee, or freeze. When it is not working for you might be in moments of addiction where we turn our mind completely off and we have given complete control to the two-year-old. When we have moments of extreme fear that can trigger us into that part of the mind.

You will notice that the percentage of what we do on a daily basis is mostly 90% unconscious. First, I want to say that that number is generous, for a lot of folks it is 95% of what they are thinking, feeling, and doing all day. Also, to be clear, it is not all negative, many things that we do throughout the day are neutral or positive. It's just where our mind is focused at the time.

It's an interesting thing to recognize and take ownership of our thoughts. You have to dig into places that may be uncomfortable. Remember in this process that you are now the adult in the front seat helping that younger version of you to let go of the junk in the trunk.

It helps to place your attention on this being enlightening and liberating for you. As you read further make it a challenge for you to be open to what has been lurking in the recesses of your mind. Personally, I have been "in process" for many years, and who I used to be is a far cry from who I am now. I share this next story because it has been one of the most powerful transformations of my own belief system, and I know that there are so many of you all that share your own version of this story.

DUMB LITTLE BLONDE

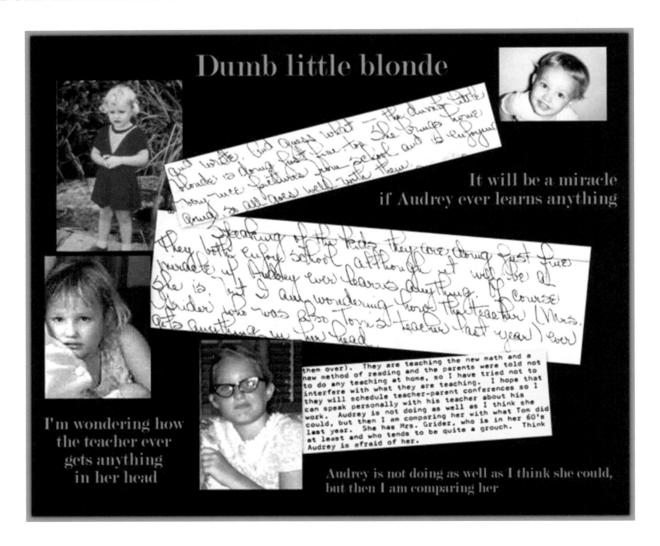

Remember when I said earlier that we don't know what we don't know? Well, growing up believing that I was stupid was just my normal. I had no reference point to know differently. I learned who I was through my environment, and I believed who I was through my mother's beliefs and perceptions.

To be fair to my mother, she really did not know any better, she had a belief about the value of boys and girls. In her eyes the boy was more important, smarter, and more capable. She didn't know what to do with a creative, mischievous, and somewhat flighty girl. She also had her own share of challenges in life. I am quite sure that being a young mother who raised two kids on her own a good portion of the time didn't leave a lot of space for introspection or mothering classes.

For me, growing up with the idea that I was stupid was a great disability. I did not do well in school, didn't have a lot of confidence, and was socially awkward. I bought the lie for so many years. I went through my Spiritual training, and they would tell me how intelligent I was, in my head I kept thinking, "not so much, but I have gotten to be cute again." I went through Hypnotherapy training and gained more knowledge of how the mind works, and still did not quite get my intelligence. It was when I started studying Science when all the tumblers fell into the correct places, and I finally realized my own unique Intelligence. That one belief alone had me driving my car in a "stupid loop" for many years.

I never would have dreamed of writing this book or doing many of the things I am able to do now if I had not owned my ability to change my thinking and perception of myself. Honestly, I believe that the most transformative moment in my life was when I understood that I was not a dumb little blonde ... I am Intelligent. That was a powerful choice point, and everything changed from there.

If you are a parent, remember to pay attention to how you are acting, speaking, and interacting with your children. Also, when you are interacting with other people in front of your kids. The little people are always in the backseat. They are learning how to be from watching your behavior. You don't have to say a word, their beliefs about who they are, how they view the world, what they are able to do in their lives, how their relationships will be are coming from you and other caretakers. The greatest lesson/belief we will ever teach our children is what Love is.

The blessing in all of this is that I used to be "stupid," I *know* that thinking. At some point I realized that I could understand science in a way that I could not before. I gained all this information and put together these tools and this book for those of us who thought we were not smart to be able to own our intelligence.

That is a part of my story, what's yours? Look at the following diagrams. Think about your own life and ponder those messages that *you* took in. This is a time for constructive change, compassion, and expansion. If you get angry with the way you took on your subconscious messages, it makes it difficult to be in the process of letting go of the belief and owning your truth. The people who raised you just did what they could with the consciousness that they had at the time. It is up to you at this choice point to own your own beliefs.

Think of it this way, this iceberg represents your mind. These are the conscious and unconscious ideas and beliefs that serve as the foundation of who you are. Perceptions are under the surface where you cannot see them, in darkness. These thoughts and beliefs are what I said earlier, "you don't know that you don't know."

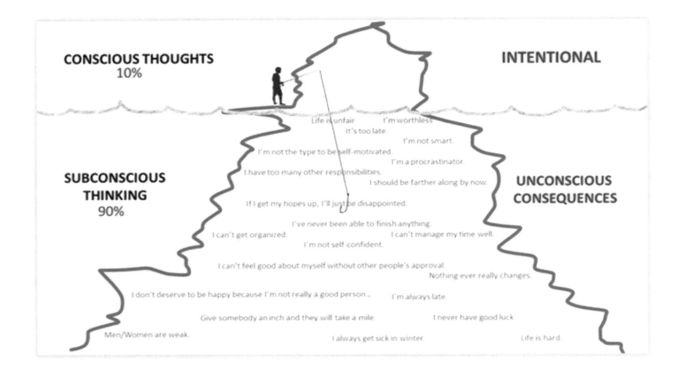

On a great road trip there could be some fishing, and your task is to think of yourself as a fisherperson. You are throwing your line in the water intending to bring in some FISH, False Ideas Sabotaging Happiness. When you bring the FISH up to the surface, in the light of day, you are able to see it clearly. Then, you do what I did the day I caught 13 fish, I let them go recognizing that they were not going to serve my best interests. When you do this, you are going from being unaware that you are unaware, to being aware of what you have been thinking from. This opens you up to being more intentional with your choices.

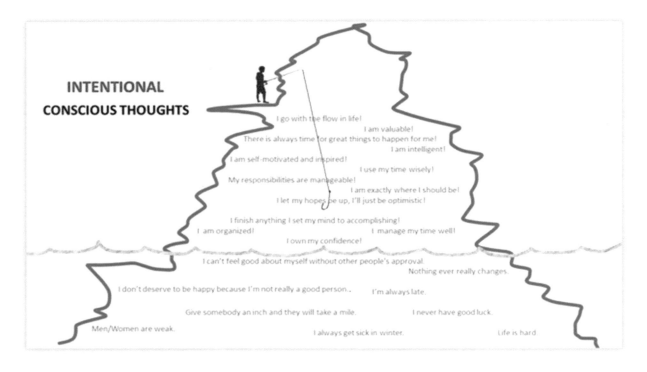

As you can see from the difference in the two diagrams, regarding how we use the fisherperson analogy, you gain more clarity by changing your unconscious thinking to the thoughts that support your version of a more balanced and happy life. This is all a process, and as I have discovered with myself, I'll probably continue to fish so I can recognize my FISH till the day I no longer inhabit this body.

THE GREATEST BELIEF

Think about your car, imagine that you have a younger you in the back seat. That version of you is still learning how to be. You as the current driver have the ability to let that younger self know what you are now learning. Your inner child is listening, they are still growing, and they are able to accept new beliefs. As you challenge your old beliefs and own your conscious thoughts, remember that little person in the back seat, let them know who they have become.

The little self hears: "You are so cute, sweet, brave, smart, interesting, valuable, funny, clever, brave, strong, etc..." The inner child takes this on as truth.

This is LOVE ... Life Of Vibrant Evolution.

The little self also hears: "You are so lazy, stupid, boring, fat, ugly, mean, weak, worthless, boring, selfish, annoying, etc..." The inner child takes this on as truth.

This is **FEAR** ... False Evidence Appearing Real.

Relative to our children or any children with whom we would interact, our one dominant intention would be to give them a conscious understanding of how powerful and important and valuable and perfect they are. Every word that would come out of our mouths would be a word that would be offered with the desire to help this individual know that they are powerful. It would be a word of empowerment. We would set the Tone for upliftment and understand that everything will gravitate to that Tone if we would maintain it consistently.
~Abraham, Ester and Jerry Hicks

FEELINGS, POWERING THE NAVIGATIONAL SYSTEM

Remember the Navigation System, Intention, Attention and Perception?

Feelings are what bring that all into action. In order to know more about how that happens, it is important to know how emotions and feelings create within and outside of your body.

I appreciate the information that HeartMath.org has to say on this subject, and instead of giving you my version, here are a few quotes for you.

"Research at the HeartMath Institute has shown that one of the most powerful factors that affect our heart's changing rhythm is our feelings and emotions."

"In general, emotional stress—including emotions such as anger, frustration, and anxiety—gives rise to heart rhythm patterns that appear irregular and erratic: the HRV waveform looks like a series of uneven, jagged peaks (an example is shown in the figure below). Scientists call this an incoherent heart rhythm pattern. Physiologically, this pattern indicates that the signals produced by the two branches of the ANS (Automatic Nervous System) are out of sync with each other. This can be likened to driving a car with one foot on the gas pedal (the sympathetic nervous system) and the other on the brake (the parasympathetic nervous system) at the same time—this creates a jerky ride, burns more gas, and isn't great for your car, either! Likewise, the incoherent patterns of physiological activity associated with stressful emotions can cause our body to operate inefficiently, deplete our energy, and produce extra wear and tear on our whole system. This is especially true if stress and negative emotions are prolonged or experienced often.

In contrast, positive emotions send a very different signal throughout our body. When we experience uplifting emotions such as appreciation, joy, care, and love; our heart rhythm pattern becomes highly ordered, looking like a smooth, harmonious wave. This is called a coherent heart rhythm pattern. When we are generating a coherent heart rhythm, the activity in the two branches of the ANS is synchronized and the body's systems operate with increased efficiency and harmony. It's no wonder that positive emotions feel so good—they actually help our body's systems synchronize and work better." ~HeartMath Institute Science

There are so many other sources that have been added to my inner library of information on the subject. HeartMath.org is a well-founded starting point to learn on the subject. They make it interesting, easy to understand, and they offer solutions for optimal Heart Health. I also like that they incorporate helping the global community through Synchronized Care Focus, a form of intentional prayer.

YOUR SMART HEART

Let's get to the greatest part of you … your physical heart.

♡ Your heart produces electromagnetic energy every second. That energy/vibration talks to the trillions of cells that make up you.

♡ Each one of those cells is intelligent, and science now knows that each cell is basically Its own little universe of energy. It reacts to the energy that your heart puts out.

♡ The heart and body hold in memory all the feelings that we have ever felt, and it is our job to recognize those feelings and put the painful ones to rest, learn from the hurt and use that information to recognize the unconscious beliefs that we harbor.

♡ The heart has a continual conversation going with the mind/brain.

♡ We perceive something, it triggers a thought, that brings about a feeling, and we go around the loop all day with either in internal harmony or discord.

♡ Your heart has its own brain, and when the head brain is connected with the heart brain all kinds of magical things happen.

Why is all this so important?

That "conversation" that your heart, mind and body are having is creating your life. The feeling of love will attract more love to your life. The feeling of appreciation will help develop more abundance/success and the level of happiness that you will manifest. Feelings can literally generate the health of your body.

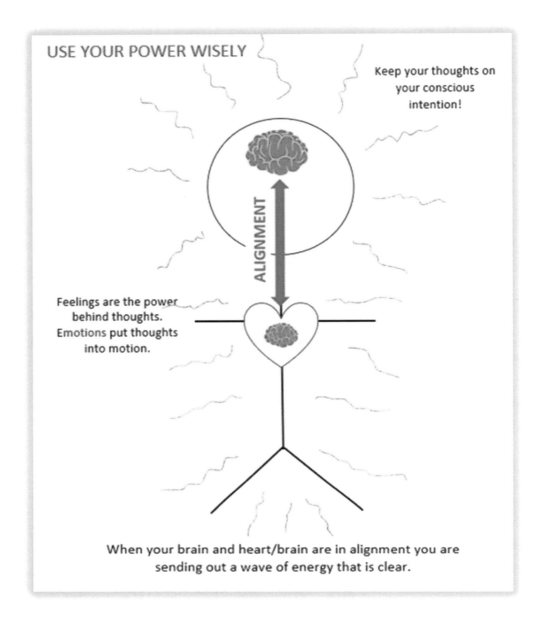

"We're simply reminded that the "stuff" that underlies all of creation is a malleable essence that reflects what we feel! So, what we choose to create, we must first feel as a reality. If we can feel it in our hearts—not just think it, but also really feel it—then it's possible in our lives!" ~Gregg Braden

In addition to pumping the blood of life within our bodies, we may think of the heart as a belief-to-matter translator. It converts the perceptions of our experiences, beliefs, and imagination into the coded language of waves that communicate with the world beyond our bodies." ~Gregg Braden

Our heart and mind are talking to the Intelligent Universe! Think about that! It is such an intelligent energy field that it responds to you! It does not discern the difference between what you do want and what you don't want, it's just always saying YES! Have to say, this bit of information was another one of the most important discoveries in my transformation journey.

To put it simply, when your heart and mind are in alignment, you are consciously creating, driving with intention, more apt to hit the destination. When you are out of alignment, wanting great things but feeling despair and hopeless, you will be more prone to take those detours, the ones that lead to rocky roads.

The vibrational feelings that your heart is putting out are programming into your intelligent navigational system.

THINKING + FEELING LOVE = BOUNDLESS DESTINATION
THINKING + FEELING FEAR = NIGHTMARE DESTINATION

"When you are aligned to fear, that becomes your truth. You know yourself through that fear and you blame yourself unknowingly for its wake and that creates more difficulty." ~Paul Selig, Channeling, 2011

So, when you feel fear, you create from fear, and you move into unconscious consequences. When you feel your power of love, and create from intention, you are more inclined to manifest your desired destination.

We all experience what I call FEAR (False Evidence Appearing Real) feelings, many people may not admit to it, even to themselves. I just cannot express enough how many people I've worked with who have shut down their feelings to the point of a deep depression or addiction issues. Sometimes as the feelings are pushed down it is too much to deal with and drugs or alcohol are a form of anesthetizing ourselves to the hurt. I genuinely believe that one of the biggest lessons we can teach our children is how to be with our feelings in a constructive way, to communicate and work through the traumas that life will present.

We are designed to feel challenging feelings. It is part of our "warning system," to let us know that there is something to be aware of. Interesting to know, we are not designed to *LIVE* in with fear all day every day. As you look at the effects on our bodies, you will see why it's important to understand what's happening inside the body when fear takes over.

- When you feel fear feelings, the amygdala, a small control center in your brain will send a signal to your Autonomic Nervous System. This sends a message to your body, that will affect your heart rate, blood pressure, digestion and elimination, and even your sexual arousal.

- Your breathing will quicken.

- Then stress hormones such as adrenaline and cortisol get released. This creates a lot of energy moving inside your body.

- The blood and energy then flow away from your heart center and towards the extremities, your arms and legs get ready for action. Moving you into the flight, fight mode.

- Ultimately, this causes the brain to shut down as the body prepares for action.

- The brain's center for reasoning and judgment becomes impaired when the amygdala senses fear, so thinking about the next best move in a crisis can be extremely hard to do.

🙁 You may even experience the sensation of time slowing down, feeling like you have tunnel vision, or that what is happening isn't real. These symptoms can make it hard to stay grounded, centered and focused in a dangerous situation.

Your body was designed to do all this to save your life in a moment of terror. The problem is that now most of us are living in a continual state of fear. Our bodies are tired, worn out and not equipped to deal with the constant physical demands of fear feelings. This continual bombardment will greatly affect your health and the positive movement of your life going forward if not checked.

WHATS FEAR GOT TO DO WITH IT

We have been taught what to fear. From when we were young, we learned that certain things were all right, and many things were not. Remember, we were in the back seat and learning everything from the people around us. We did not come into this lifetime afraid of anything.

We learned to be frightened of doing something wrong, we might get beaten.
Scared of the water, we may drown or get eaten by sharks.
Fearful of the dark, there might be something out there that will hurt us.
Afraid of running too fast, we might fall and get hurt.
Terrified of the world ending, apocalypse type stuff … I might not live to be 30!
Afraid of loving, they may leave and break my heart.
Terrified of death, going to hell or the void of nothingness.

We also learned to be afraid of other people, be afraid of strangers; do not talk to people you don't know. We have been taught that there's people out there that want to hurt you. On the other end of the spectrum, we have also been taught that there are people out there to help you, that you should trust them and follow blindly. Then, when that trust is blown it turns into a whole new level of fear feelings. This is a process of checking all of our beliefs, about everything.

Don't get me wrong, there are people out there that do want to harm other people, but we do not have to be afraid ahead of time that people are going to hurt us. When you envision the possible scenario ahead of time and imagine from fearfull thoughts, you are plugging in an unconscious program to the navigation. When you imagine a positive outcome then you set an intentional "preset" program. This will help you to circumvent the unconscious fight, flight, freeze. Freezing when someone might want to hurt you is not the best option. If it happens that you do find yourself in a situation where someone wants to do harm, you certainly should be conscious. Use your intuition and your senses to be aware if danger is approaching.

Many times, on my Soulitude camping trips, I notice my environment and check to see if there is any reason to be afraid. In those moments I check myself ahead of anything happening and imagine what I would do to keep myself safe. That way my fight, flight or freeze is already set on my actions. Being consciously prepared is much safer than being afraid.

People think things like, "I don't want to lose my job, I really don't want to get cancer, I'm too old, I won't find a good partner for me at this age, etc. …" And then they are surprised when it happens! You know this is true! We have all seen it happen to ourselves and others all the time. A big part of this process is to train yourself to recognize when these unconscious future predictions come up and be able to take another road in your mind.

We do not have to look into the future and imagine all the possibilities that could possibly happen in life. Somebody might hurt you, you might lose your job, you might get too fat, or you might get ill. On your conscious road trip, take things as they come and focus your full attention on what solutions and tools you can apply. Reroute and get back on the road that has your intention attached to it.

CONNECT, NAVIGATE WITH FEELINGS

Many of us have a disconnect with our emotions and feelings. I know for myself that I pushed down, hid from, and ignored my feelings to such an extent that it took years to allow them to the surface so that I could deal with them. Especially anger, hurt, loneliness, and feeling ashamed. In my world growing up, these things were not to be discussed, it simply was not all right to express my pain. If I was angry my mother would have told me that she would give me something to be angry about, that meant a serious spanking … with anything she could find … a belt or wooden spoon was common. So, I learned how to silence myself. Remember, my mother also had her own beliefs of how to raise kids, I don't blame her at this point or hold onto the feelings that her behavior caused. More about how to let go of these things coming up in the Timeline and Victimization Loop.

When I was in training to become a Practitioner at Agape, I had a situation that made me incredibly angry, and because of my lack of communication skills I just didn't say anything to the person that I was angry with. I had a strong belief that I would just deal with it myself, usually by ignoring the offending behavior. Many times, I would just let go of a relationship instead of dealing with the issue. Honestly, this is by far one of the most common challenges that clients deal with.

Thank goodness for the guidance of the Practitioner I was working with at the time. When I shared the story with her, she gave me the guidance that I needed to shift my perception and thinking so that I could find a way to work through my anger.

In the session I told her that I knew I should not be angry, that I should perceive it differently and move into an alignment with just forgiving the situation and letting it go. She said quite the opposite, she said that it was all right to feel angry, and it's what you do when you're angry that is important. Then, she shared some ideas that were new to me and some tools to use so that I would process through my anger. I believe that this was the first time in my life that I ever knew that it was alright to have those kinds of feelings and be able to address them with another person. That was the first time I felt the permission to be angry! I could give my anger a voice and let go of being the victim of other people's behavior.

Let's take a minute here to specifically talk about anger. Anger is one of the few feelings that can be on the Fear and the Power side. The trick is to make sure that you are coming from a *righteous anger* instead of a victim anger. Victim anger is being at the effect of someone/something, and you have no power to change it. Righteous anger is understanding that you have been at the effect of something/someone, you recognize it, and are now using that energy of anger to change the circumstances. You are taking constructive action to overcome the challenge. Much of the time using effective communication can help with this.

Allow for *your* challenging feelings. Bring them up slowly and with compassion and understanding. Pay attention to them, you are working *through* the challenge so that you can own your power on the other side.

When you are feeling what I call "Fear Feelings," they are your guide.

Think of your fear like you're getting a call from your EGO (the kid in the backseat) saying, "Hey, you have an old program running here, time to hit the brakes, go through the construction zone, and input a new belief system! This part of the game is learning how to be with your feelings in a way that is constructive, not destructive. Allow all your feelings to lead the way, they are a large part of your greatest strength.

Your thinking will take you far, and your feelings will take you even further. Your feelings move your token around the board. Which of the following feelings do you spend most of your time in?

False Evidence Appearing Real

FRUSTRATED	EXASPERATED	**APPRECIATION**	EXUBERANT
EMBARRASSED	HOSTILE	LOVING	GIDDY
UNEASY	BITTER	JOY	EAGER
WORRIED	PESSIMISTIC	GRATEFUL	ANIMATED
TERRIFIED	LONELY	HAPPY	PLAYFUL
NERVOUS	RESENTFUL	DELIGHTED	PASSIONATE
PANICKY	DISGUSTED	BLISSFUL	INVIGORATED
JITTERY	ANNOYED	CONFIDENT	ENERGIZED
HORRIFIED	DISAPPOINTED	OPTIMISTIC	PEACEFUL
ANXIOUS	ASHAMED	EXCITED	CONTENT
LONELY	OVERWHELMED	INSPIRED	RELAXED
SUSPICIOUS	DISCOURAGED	ENERGETIC	SECURE
APPREHENSIVE	RAGE	ENTHUSIASTIC	COMPOSED
FRIGHTENED	APATHETIC	INTERESTED	RELIEVED
JEALOUS	DEPRESSED	UPBEAT	COMFORTABLE
UNNERVED	GRIEF	PEACEFUL	C A L M

Life Of Vibrant Evolution

CALM IS A CHOICE

Ideally, most of us would like to go from being anxious to happy, from angry to loving, or from sad to delighted. For most of us this isn't what happens, it's just too big of a jump, especially if we have been in those intense hard feelings for a long time. One option that we have the power to do is choose calm. That is at the bottom of the chart on the LOVE side for a reason. It's the ground floor and a good starting point to go up the emotional ladder of feeling better.

Calm is always a choice. Always. At times it is not an easy thing to do. I get it, in the midst of chaos our natural response is to be stressed, anxious, angry, etc.

This is one of the most important things that I will say in this book… **The more we make the choice to be present and focus on being calm, the easier it is to get to the solutions.**

One more thing about being calm, it must be authentic. You can't just say, "I'm calm" and there you have it. You must be in the feeling of calm; heart rate down, breath rate down, muscles more relaxed, feeling leveled out. Too many times I see people saying that they are calm, when clearly, they are presenting in all their body language that they are far from the kingdom of Calm. Just saying it doesn't make it so. Be aware of your body language, you may be fooling yourself.

These are some of the many reasons to begin the practice of choosing calm.

∞ The more we choose calm, the more ingrained we make that feeling as our new habit, our "normal homeostasis."

∞ When we are in a calm state all the prior symptoms of fear feelings are almost the opposite. We have much more control over our body and brain.

∞ When you are calm it will help reduce the stress hormone known as cortisol.

∞ When you are authentically calm, your heart rate and breathing will slow down in response.

∞ The energy flows to the center of your body and you become more grounded centered and focused.

∞ You will create more dopamine and serotonin instead of adrenaline.

∞ Your thinking becomes more clear, focused, and expansive!

∞ As you own your ability to choose calm, the more life is aligned emotionally, the more physically healthy, and in time, happier.

EXERCISE FOR CREATING A DEEPER CALM

I find in my own moments that I need a calm "time out," I find a quiet place to realign. Sometimes it's easy and I just shut the door to my room or office, but other times I might be in the midst of too many people, so, my car, the bathroom or a walk around the block can be helpful. Once I am in a calmer environment, I focus on what I can to bring me back to a calmer state. My number one go to is always starting by focusing on my breath. Breathing is always a great place to start to bring your body to a state of focused calm. Your body is naturally designed to have the breath bring back balance. There is a method to breathing exercise, and at first you will want to focus more on the details of this process. Then, over time this will be a natural automatic response to stress, fear, anxiety, etc.

Get yourself in as comfortable a position as possible and focus on your breathing. With each breath in you are being present in the now moment, acknowledging "I'm breathing in calm," and allowing for the feeling of relaxed calm to be present in your physical body.

With each breath out you are being present in the now moment, letting go of the attention on the "problem," and releasing tension in the body.

Things to add to Breathing Exercise

- You may want to listen to soothing music or sounds to help with unwinding.
- I have meditations on my website, one of them is "Calm Is a Choice," and there are many other sources of calm meditations.
- Add to the mix some Aromatherapy, there are many oils that can be beneficial. I really like lavender, rose and vanilla.
- Ask for support from someone who will help to ground and center you.
- Remember your intention for being calm, "I choose calm so I can think more clearly and focus on my solutions..." Hold that as your mantra.

"When your mind is in a state of love, your brain releases hormones such as oxytocin (the love hormone), serotonin which causes the body to be calm and supports maintenance of the body's tissues and organs, and growth hormone which regenerates the body's structures. In contrast, when your mind is in fear, the brain releases a completely different set of hormones into the blood and profoundly changes the fate of the cells and the body. The stress hormone, cortisol, shuts down growth and invests the body's energy into protection, it also shuts off the immune system to conserve energy for fight and flight. Stress also causes the release of both norepinephrine that suppresses body maintenance, and histamine, which engages defense mechanisms. Your mind is the chemist. The words you say in your mind release the chemistry." ~Dr. Bruce Lipton

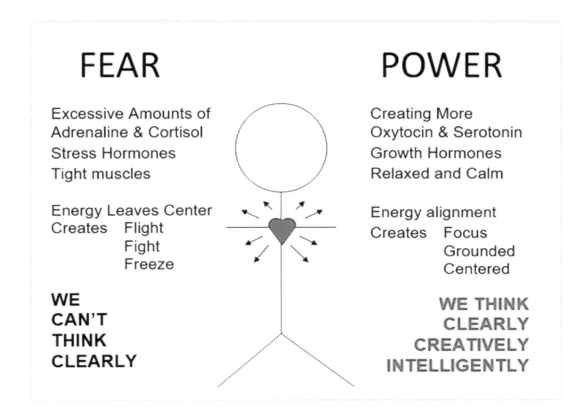

Our heart creates electromagnetic energy.
The energetic vibration "talks" to our TRILLIONS of INTELLIGENT cells.
The cells "hear" a message based on either Love or Fear feelings.
When you're at least authentically calm you own your power to consciously choose the road best traveled.
The vibration that your body "hears" from the energy of calm is powerful.

FEAR INTO POWER

YOUR CHOICE

This is the tool to change and possess your mind.

This exercise is where the rubber meets the road, and you get to find out why you ever went down the hill to hell in the first place. This is the prime place to find those hidden beliefs that are sabotaging your life.

This Tool is designed to investigate and ponder your thoughts and feelings in a constructive way. You will use that new information about you to forge a new path in your mind for what you would rather be doing. In a profound way, this is creating a new neuro-road in your mind/brain. With this tool you will be using the critical thinking part of your mind that is questioning the source of things, investigating, and using logic, deduction and reason. This is to determine what the subconscious thoughts are, where they came from in your timeline, and how they came to be your "navigational system."

These beliefs are always from the programing 0-8 years in your timeline, or from an experience, or from both. Many times, it is from both the program and experience, as you learned the program and created some experience from that belief.

With this Fear Into Power Tool, you are basically in the process of hypnotizing yourself and owning your power to transform those limiting beliefs that you took on early in life. Remember in the gameboard The Pit Stop when you have to address those fear feelings? This is the part of the game where you get to process *through* challenging feelings in a productive way. When you are feeling any fear feeling, this is the "communication" that you have with yourself to sort things out and get back to the great business of life.

Here is how it works … Use a notebook make two columns like you see below.
When you are angry, worried, anxious, etc. you write it down on the FEAR side.
Where is your attention? What are those challenging thoughts that keep zipping around in your mind?

In this process you are asking yourself questions that will bring about the answers to your unconscious thinking and behavior. I like to call this part of the journey, **Positive Pondering**. You explore your history and begin to understand the thoughts in your mind and your habits/behavior.

Important questions to ask yourself are:

? Is what is happening now something that I learned in the 0-8 years of early programming in my life?

? Is this something that has been taken on unconsciously through an experience?

- What is the challenge, why am I feeling bad?
- Commit to the process of investigation, what happened to create this.
- Intentionally choose to *be* calm so you can think clearly.
- Set and own a new intention.
- Create power statements to use as your new way of thinking, the new pathway in your mind.
- It is a process … be patient with yourself.
- Be compassionate and allow for change.

POWER STATEMENTS

At this point, the fear side is working, now on to your Power. This is the part of the process where you are creating a new place for your attention to be focused. You get to define a clear direct perception of who you are and where you are choosing to go.

A Power Statement is what holds the place for you to go forward into. It is the strong declaration you are making about the direction of your life. When you create a power statement you are redirecting the pathways from our mind from an unconscious thinking pattern to a conscious determined road of direct course.

You are declaring what you choose as your inner and outer path in life. it Make your statements firm, and with deep conviction.

Think about the fears that you acknowledged, the power statement would be the opposite of whatever you wrote there. You will see some examples of this coming up.

I have had many clients who were anxious much of the time, when they looked at their Fears around this, they could see the program in the 0-8 with influential people demonstrating anxiety, and then in the experiences of life they had many moments of extreme anxiety into panic. They could also see that a lot of the anxiety started with a statement like, "what if," which means that they were not being present in the moment and focused on intentional living. A lot of the time I will have them question their anxiety and ask themselves, "Is this true." Most of the time, probably not. It's always interesting to find out how much of what they are anxious about actually happened.

For a person with anxiety like this, the power statements could be like these.

- ★ I am present in each moment, focused on the good that life has to give.
- ★ In any given moment I own my truth!
- ★ I Am grounded, centered, focused and calm!

And remember, when you are saying and feeling the power statement, you are the adult in the front seat, letting the kid know that you've got the wheel and are in charge. You are having a conversation with them about the situation and understanding why you would be feeling like that and most importantly calming their fear with the awareness of you, the adult, taking the wheel of your car with confidence, strength and constructive action.

When you use your power statements as your new guide, you are not following the path that may have been set by your parents, teachers, or the environment. You are forging your own new way with intention and purpose.

When you are creating your Power Statements follow these guidelines:

- ✊ Use "I language" for your Power Statement.
    - o   I AM … I KNOW … I HAVE …
- ✊ Keep it short and simple.
- ✊ Your power statements declare that this "thing" is already happening!
- ✊ Write it in the present tense, in the here-and-now.
    - o   RIGHT NOW, TODAY!
- ✊ Make the vocabulary personal to YOU.
    - o   Use words that touch you at the feeling level.
- ✊ State WHAT you want, not HOW I will manifest it.
- ✊ Be specific with the qualities not quantities of what you are creating.
    - o   I am abundant and generate lots of money from known and unknown sources!
- ✊ State WHAT but not HOW.
- ✊ Your statement should be in the present tense, it is happening now.
- ✊ Within the Intelligent Universe you are putting your intentions into the act of creation. Know this and act as if your power statement is already manifested in your life, as if it is already in the works!

If you think about the power statements with the Road Trip, imagine that while you're driving, you will say…

"Siri, get me directions, I'm going to my best job ever!"
"Hey Google, my best and highest is happening right now, directions please."
"I'm meeting my soul partner that's just right for me, plug it in Maps!"
Do you get my drift? All the intelligence that we use on our devices is the same thing that we are able to do for ourselves. We are "talking" to the "internet" all the time.

Remember, *feeling* is what will get you around the board. When owning your power statement, the words are significant, but the feeling that they create is even more important. I understand that many of us have suppressed feelings, and it can be a chore to get back in touch with something that we may not consider to be safe.

There are beliefs around how you may feel if you open the "Pandoras Box."

You may start crying and never stop, you may not know how to control the rage and do something regrettable. Maybe you don't want other people to think you are weak with such feelings. Like my story, sometimes certain feelings just are not OK. The reasons to keep emotions in check are varied, and unique to you. One thing is for sure, just because you keep them locked up in the vault doesn't mean that they are not affecting your life.

The words we speak out loud and in the silence of our mind set the path on the road of life, the feelings put energy into that navigation to set your path and make your goal happen. It is not just changing your thoughts; you are owning the full intention of the new statement and the feelings behind it.

Here are some key points to own in order to reach the destination.

- ✓ You must believe in what you are saying, have the trust and faith that it is already in the works.
- ✓ Feel the excitement, the enthusiasm or appreciation of what you're manifesting!
- ✓ Know what actions you have to take to get to your destination.
- ✓ You will have to continually focus on the intention of your statements.
- ✓ You must trust that it is already happening.

Here are 10 mindful intentional power statements that will change your life. Hold them as true, own the feelings of appreciation, enthusiasm, excitement, or even just being consciously calm and sure.

- ∞ I live in the present moment.
    Every moment is an opportunity to be focused on what you can do to make your life better.
    Each challenge is a new choice point to find the solutions to make the next minute better.
- ∞ I use my feelings as a guide to my conscious choices.
    If you are feeling from what I call "fear feelings" like anger, anxiety, stress, or worry, you are not thinking as clearly as you could. You are also at the effect of an unconscious belief. Those feelings are your guide that it is time to stop and re-evaluate what's going on at the moment.

∞ I focus on the solutions to any challenging situation.

> We have been trained to focus on the problems in life, and unfortunately where we place our attention is what we will get. I know that times get rough, and it is natural to tell your friends, family and co-workers what's going on with you. The problem is that when you tell it to too many people and spend all that time and energy on the problem, you will continue to focus on what has or could happen that is bad rather than the possible great outcome. Just this one power statement alone is seriously life changing.

∞ I learn from the past and use the wisdom to make conscious new intentional choices.

> The past is not meant to define you … it is just where your consciousness was at the time. You learned how to do what you did, and if it is no longer working for you, you get to learn a new way to be. It's just that simple.

∞ I let go of judgement and allow compassion to lead the way.

> If I could say that in my therapy practice that there would be one major thing that many people do that makes their lives difficult, it would be dealing with constant judgement. We judge or get judged by something that happened years ago, and that will be forever how we look at that person. Or we judge without even knowing the circumstances of people's lives. We judge and do the thing that we are judging. We hurt with all the judgement, and there is no room for letting go. Compassion for the unconsciousness of who they (and you) have been is the key to everything. Then, set healthy boundaries, using effective communication and a focus on solutions. This will move your life in a powerful direction.

∞ Divine right action is taking place in my life all the time.

> I know that this one might be a bit of a challenge. One thing I have seen for all these years of working with clients, the hard times are where we learn and from the lessons, we discover our power. Life is all about the journey and the contrasts along the way. When you put this power statement out ahead of you then this is more of what you will own in the great moments and the difficult times ahead.

∞ Abundance comes to me from known and unknown sources. My life is rich.

> This one is pretty amazing; I have witnessed so many miracles in my own life and in the lives of my clients over the years. For many of us we grew up with what I call lack and limitation beliefs, if that is the case with you, it might be that this statement is difficult to own. This would be a good opportunity to look at your beliefs around money, success, and abundance.

∞ I continually and consciously let go of what no longer serves me.

> If it makes you unhappy, unhealthy, feeling unloved or lacking, it might not serve you anymore. Time to let go and move on to better things.

∞ I continue to lean into the people who support, appreciate, and respect me. I live in love.

> This does not mean you have to get rid of those who are not supportive, disrespectful or have a lack of appreciation. It just means that you will spend your time with those who resonate with the best and highest that you are creating in your life. Some good constructive communication will help to create better relationships with those that are not in alignment with this power statement.

∞ I live in deep appreciation for all that was, all that Is, and all that will ever be.

> The feeling of appreciation is one of the most powerfully creative feelings. Feel gratitude for where you have been, for what you are doing and for what you are wanting. This will make all things better in your world.

REVEAL BURIED BELIEFS

If there is a part of you that feels bad or says no every time you say your Power Statement ask yourself, "What do I really believe about this? Is this another person's belief that I no longer wish to own? Is this something that doesn't hold any value for me anymore?"

When thinking of the car analogy, imagine that all these old beliefs are in the trunk of your car, weighing you down, causing the car to not go fast enough or with strong direction. Sometimes it can get so heavy back there that it is dragging on the ground and the car stops dead in its tracks.

MIND ROAD TRIP FOR DUMPING THE TRUNK

- ∞ Focus your attention on a belief you have that you are ready to let go of.
  - It could be anything; what part of your life are you ready to upgrade?
- ∞ What purpose does your belief serve?
- ∞ If you no longer need it, you have this opportunity to give it up, are you ready to make the commitment to yourself?
- ∞ Imagine your life without this belief.
- ∞ Then create a power statement that is in alignment with what you want and put a higher vibration feeling into it.

Make sure that you take the time to do these, it is all a part of the game. As with any game, you have to be in the process to get the prize.

INTENTION EXERCISE:

Set five intentions, five things that you have been meaning to do.

Create five power statements to support the intentions.

What creative action can I do to make them stick in my mind?

- Take a piece of paper and write your statement on it, then put it up on the inner part of a cabinet door, or your mirror, maybe the inside of the visor on your car. Any place where you will look occasionally and take note.
- You can make a song or a mantra out of your Power Statements. *"I'm grounded, focused, centered and calm"* is a favorite of mine.
- Look yourself in the eye when you are getting ready for the day at say it out loud to yourself in the mirror. Make it fun!

In the photo below is an example of how this process has worked in my own life. This was a few years ago when I was having a hard time. I went on my very first solo camping trip and had to take the time to really figure out why things were the way that they were for me. I will never forget sitting down at the table in the middle of a ring of redwood trees, writing this, working through the stuff, and coming to this realization. This truly was a life changing moment for me, and there are times where I still go back to this power statement.

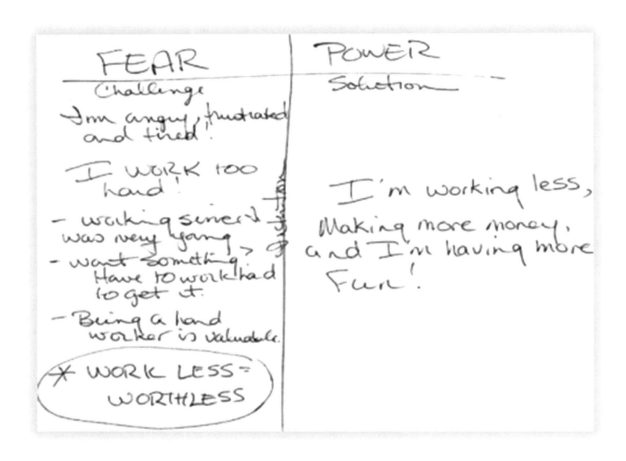

Over the years I have talked with many people who have felt challenged about money, they work too hard, and deeply feel a lack of appreciation. If this has ever been your situation, feel free to adopt this power statement for yourself.

Just notice when the resistance shows up … because it will.

You will doubt yourself. You will worry. You will have to pull back the layers of your beliefs, to own your truth. And then, thank goodness, you will level up when you do all of that. With all this in action, life will get a bit easier and better day by day.

I have to say, this is absolutely a process. Owning that affirmation did not happen overnight. I am so thankful for the Fear Into Power tool, I am still using it when I have a big challenge. This is the main process that has brought me more alignment with my power than fear. It has been the most effective tool for so many of my clients as well.

You can use this format for many situations that come up in life. I have shared it many times with people who are debating a big change in their life. Pros or cons to move, to make a career change, have a baby, etc. … It helps to map the future.

PLAN OF CREATIVE ACTION

FEAR	POWER
CHALLENGE	SOLUTION
ADDICTION	RECOVERY
CONS	PROS
STRESSED	CALM
OLD HABITS	NEW INTENTIONS
HATEFUL	LOVING

Below is an example of what I did for my New Year's visioning process.

You can see how I processed what I learned from the old year and how I gained clarity on the intentions for the new year.

No More of This | Intention, Focus and Solutions

Unhealthy relationships.
Why?

I am the love of my life.
I draw people to me that love me.
People in my life are supportive, fun and loving.

What was my part?

What was my attention on?

I am valuable.
The relationships that I create are respectful, considerate, patient, compassionate, cooperative and kind.

Why would I choose that?

I am all those things I wish to have in a great relationship.

What do I really want?

I communicate effectively and forgive easily.

Not healthy, not enough energy.
Why?

I love and honor my body.
I make healthy choices that support the health of my body.

Did I make choices that supported my body?

My attention is on the solutions that create energy and well-being.

What was my attention on?
Did I spend too much time focused on negative feelings and experiences?

I work through my feelings that don't support an environment of calm.
I spend my time focused on intentional living and making healthy choices.

I was working with a client, and they were having a moment with their business. Things were not bad; they were just in a moment of being somewhat stuck. The expectations of where they thought they would be at this point were just not being met. The business took off very well, and things had been moving in the right direction. This business had come to a point where it could either really take off, or not. While we were talking, it became apparent that there was some unconscious thinking and feeling going on and it was not being addressed. There was worry, some stress of unresolved issues, and anxiety about possible future problems. All of it was fixable, and none of it was "true" at the moment. It is just where the attention had unconsciously gone to.

Remember, for most of us, much of what we are thinking and feeling throughout the days is not paid attention to. We just have this "normal" feeling of worry, anxiety, stress, etc., and it is just a part of our day. We have been trained to believe it's normal. Notice how many people around you continually talk about how bad things are, or how bad things might get. It is how we have learned to relate to each other. It is the program; they don't even realize that they're doing it.

Years ago, I had a client that was having a challenge with a business partner. The partner had a lot of anxiety, stress and worry about what he thought was happening with the business. I gave my client the task of going back to their business partner and showing them the following diagram, he was to explain how the Fear into Power process works. Then, working together as a team they were to look at the issues from a new perspective, understand the unconscious focus of attention, then decide on what new thoughts and actions they could take. Happy to say that it worked, and the team was able to work through the issues and into the next stage of their success. When you fully learn this process and use all the tools, it can be beneficial to share with the people around you, just make sure they are interested. I had to learn the hard way to only share my information with people who wanted to know more. When you do share with friends or family it helps to solidify the information in your own daily practice, it also creates better communication, cooperation, and collaboration. It is a great team builder, and everyone gets to level up together. Below is the format that I gave them to share with their pit crew.

INTENTION	PERCEPTION	ATTENTION
What's Working?	What's the Challenge?	What's the Solution?
Write down the things that are working; anything that is in your favor. What gives you a reason to want to continue doing what you're doing?	Write down the fear feelings that come up. Are you worried? Maybe you're dealing with anxiety, stress or anger? Are there people who you are not communicating with that require some constructive conversation? Is it time for a new clearer vision, or time to take a new direction? This is the place where you own your tools that bring you the clarity... Meditation, Visualization and Prayer.	There is always a solution. It might not be the one that you expect, or one that seems like it will be the best in the long run. If it seems like a viable option in the moment and it feels better, consider going there.

Taking the time to work through the issues with conscious intention always moves things toward a better outcome. Instead of the fear unconsciously running the show, you are bringing it to the surface and acknowledging your ability to change it. Most importantly you are gaining clarity, insight, and focusing on the solutions as a team.

I have seen too many times where a problem was just an idea in the imagination of many a client, it was never much of a surprise when months later they would share with me that they lost their job, are going through a divorce or without a favorite friend. The unconscious attention won. When you keep complaining about what you do not want, you get what you don't want. It is just that simple.

The Timeline tool coming up will help you to sort through the subconscious beliefs and where they came from. Keep on the road and be kind and patient with yourself. Also, appreciate that you have chosen to come this far on your journey.

CHOICE POINT TIMELINE

The last of the human freedoms, to choose one's attitude in any given set
of circumstances is to choose one's own way." ~Victor Frankel

If you find you're here and now intolerable and it makes you unhappy, you have three
options; remove yourself from the situation, change it or accept it totally.
Eckhart Tolle, The Power of Now

It is one thing to do the Fear into Power exercise, it will absolutely move you in the right direction. It makes it even more effective when you add in the Choice Point Timeline. This tool shows the patterns of your life, it gives a new and clearer perspective. When you see the past from a greater viewpoint and you take out the judgement, then you are able to bring up the "stuff" from the bottom of the iceberg into the light of day and constructively address it.

Using the Choice Point Timeline is one of the most effective tools to use for getting out of an unconscious habit. It gives you the ability to see the sabotaging and destructive behavior and begin the process of owning your choice on how you transform your life. This process helps to reveal the lies we tell ourselves and reinforce every single day. With this you get to be your own private detective to get to the truth of your life. Basically, you use this to see the pattern of beliefs and behavior that has brought you to this point in life.

The quality of events surrounding you in any given moment in time may be reflecting specific beliefs that you hold in that moment of time. ~Gregg Braden

Imagine that those belief systems that are no longer serving you are hidden in a lovely treasure chest somewhere on your timeline. If you really want to find where your hidden treasures are, look for the things that still embarrass you about your childhood. I have this thing that was one of my most embarrassing things that I did as a kid. I had an addiction to sugar. I was young and ignorant and did not realize it was a problem. All I knew is that there was a program running that said, "I must have sugar."

Let's define what that "program" I was running really means in my life … when I went out Trick or Treating, I would get ½ of a pillowcase of candy. It was eaten within three days. Seriously. Then I have the worst story, and this is the one that I would get teased about well into my adult life. If there were no cookies, fudge, ice cream, etc., in the house I would get a box of brown sugar along with my spoon and sit on the floor of my room and eat it. Right out of the box. A lot of it. Why would I do that? This was the question that I posed for the Timeline and Fear into Power tools. I thought about that period of my life and remembered anything that stood out with regard to sugar. In my family, every single night we would have dessert after our meal, and if I had been a "bad girl," there would be no desert for me. So, sweet sugar turned into my go to for feeling better, the moments of sweet satisfaction were my happy moments. Then, pondering it further, there came that time when had the desire to not be fat and I had to curb the sugar. Trust me, I found another dysfunctional habit to replace sugar.

When I finally did my Timeline, along with the Fear into Power tool, that is when all the cylinders fell into place, and I was able to understand my dysfunctional addictions for what they were … I could know what I didn't know and own the process of letting the limiting beliefs go.

When I saw where the pattern started with my addictions there was awareness. When I understood why little Audrey would have wanted to disappear into an abyss of sugar, that was the moment I could process more of the lack of worth, the "stupid" program, and all the other beliefs that I had about myself. That process has taken years of leveling up, just like climbing up one rung on a ladder after another. Each step feeling more free and lighter. I managed to get a lot of junk out of the trunk! How about you? Are you willing to look at your own Timeline? Did you say yes? Great! Move along then.

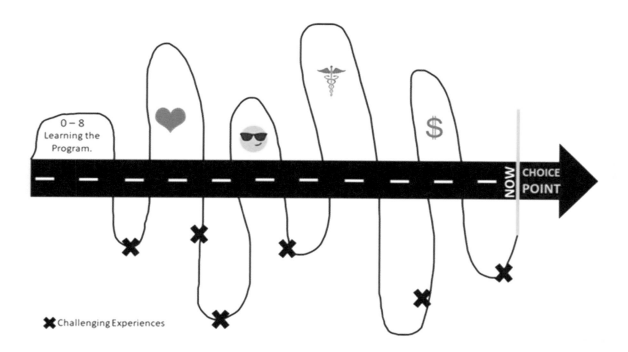

Past challenges are to be learned from.
Grow and gain the wisdom.
Then let go and release the challenging emotion.
It does not serve your intentions to dwell in negativity.
Attention on the problems will make it impossible to move forward in a positive direction.

MIND TRIP TO INCREASE CLARITY WITH THE CHOICE POINT TIMELINE

- Get out a piece of paper, poster board, or I give my clients large sheets of butcher block paper for this exercise.
- Make a line down the middle of the paper.
- Then map out the events that have happened in your life.
   - Experiences above the line are the times that worked for you. Moments that you have experienced that have made you happy, brought you success/abundance, love, etc.
   - Below the line are challenging, difficult or painful experiences.
- Recount relationships with family, friends, fellow students, co-workers etc.
- Review your health, look for patterns in illness or great health.
- Look at your success/abundance, with school, jobs, etc. When were you at your best? When were the moments that you faltered?
- What were the periods of happiness and joy. What were the moments of depression or strong fear feelings?

With each what were the highlights, the great moments? Write those above the top line. What were the challenges? Those go below the line. There is an example coming up.

- Write down the years, as close to accurate as you can.

While you are doing this exercise, ask yourself the following questions:

What lessons have I learned from my past?
What is the wisdom I have gained?
Do I keep creating the same challenges?
What beliefs might have that contribute to the unconscious patterns?
What was I thinking?
Do I still worry about what I may create the problem again?

This exercise is not designed for you to actively relive all those memories and be in the pain of those moments, it is just to get a representation of the patterns that you have created. It's like you want to be an observer of the experience from a new perspective. All those events were created with a consciousness that you are now in the process of changing. Be compassionate with yourself … and others.

COMPASSION AND UNDERSTANDING

If you want others to be happy, practice compassion.
If you want to be happy, practice compassion. ~Dalai Lama

Judgement is that thing that will drive you off the track and off to an undesirable location. It is like if you're planning a vacation, and you have it set to go to the most fun, beautiful, exciting, and relaxing vacation ever. Judgement is that thing that puts you on the breaks and leaves you stranded. You, my friend just got side lined.

Being hard on ourselves and others is all too familiar for many of us. We judge just about everything, and there is not much positive influence coming out of that judgement. We judge others for a lot of different reasons, and to somehow make ourselves feel better about our own life is probably one of the front runners.

When looking at your life, there are a lot of things that you can look at with regard to the past that can have judgement about your actions attached to it. I should have done that differently, I should have known better, I should have learned my lesson the first time, etc. You also judge what someone else should have or should not have done.

In this practice you learn to own compassion regarding the past. You did what you did with the consciousness that you had at the time. Your *learned* consciousness. Many things you would never have done with the consciousness that you are now learning to possess. If you hold onto judgement, it is just keeping the past in play. Let it go! It has done and over, and the only place that the past may still reside is in your head, your heart, or in any unconscious consequences that may still be in play. When I am working with groups in rehab, that is one of the challenging things, they are all in an unconscious consequence of being in the rehab. And … they are all able to change their experience because of the tools and reprogramming that they are receiving at the rehab. It is tricky to look at that kind of experience with appreciation and clarity, but when I see the clients understand that one aspect it can have life affirming results.

For now, be aware and notice when you do have some judgement going on. What kind of feelings does judgement bring for you? I have to say, I have spent quite a lot of my life in various forms of judgement… as my daughters can attest to. I have had to look at the feelings that judgement brought up for me, and many of them had to do with me feeling less-than, unworthy, and lonely. It didn't help that I worked in one of the most gossipy industries! Hair Designers are notorious for judgmental chatter. I have had to look at my timeline and figure out where it began, and you guessed it… I was in the backseat of Moms car, and she had been in the backseat of her mother's car. Turns out my grandmother was a very judgmental person. I'm sure it didn't start with her… she was a backseat rider as well. One thing is for sure, many of my judgements came from me judging myself the most!

Here are some examples of how judgement can look.

- Judging other people based on their appearance.
- Judging on how people act, the choices that they make.
- Judging on what people didn't do.
- Judging the amount of money or possessions other people have.
- Judging why people would be a couple, he/she too good for the other.

It's all right, we are not changing these things overnight. For now, just be patient and focus on being present with as much compassion as possible.

THE CRASH

We have all had that moment in the timeline of our lives where we hit a wall. Something happened that was traumatic, and, in that moment, we did the best that we could to survive and then move beyond it. If you think of it with the car analogy, It would be like you had an accident and it damaged your car. Sometimes it is just a fender bender, and you acquire a little dent and move on. Sometimes it is a full out collision, and our car is in bad shape. At that point we would take it into the mechanic and get it fixed, because we always need our cars to get around.

Unfortunately, in life for many of us after our traumatic crash, we never found a mechanic/therapist to help figure out how to get the dings out and put the car back into working form. So, we live with the dings and dents and keep on going. I have found that what a lot of us do is to take the pieces of us that fall off and put them in our trunk. We hide all the hurt and damage in there for no one else to see and we carry it around. After years of adding more and more of our "baggage" it weighs down the back of our car. In fact, it can start banging around back there in such a way that it makes it hard for us to drive.

Using the Timeline allows the opportunity to address past accidents in a new way and with a different perspective. Some of the work you will be able to do on your own, and for those of us that have had a big crash or more, it might be a good idea to find a therapist who can help direct you through the challenging process of letting go.

THE REARVIEW MIRROR

As you are doing the timeline process, it will give you an idea of the amount of time you are spending with your attention in the rearview mirror. Think about how you are feeling while you are looking in the past. Are you still angry, resentful, guilty, or ashamed? Are you ready to let that go? The Timeline is designed to help with all that.

"To forgive is to set a prisoner free and discover that the prisoner is you."

~Lewis B. Smedes

When you think about this quote, it basically answers the question of how important it is to forgive ourselves and others. I do not believe we can be the fullness of who we are when we are harboring resentment in our heart. Many of us have been taught to think that it is powerful when we do not forgive someone. People say they will never forgive someone, as if it will forever hurt the other person. We learn a belief about staying angry with people … "I will never forgive them for what they did," is a very common phrase and when we add "I'll get even with them" to the scenario then you can see how things will never change. Many of the wars that are taking place in the world are an extreme example of this. In my therapy practice, I'm quite sure the word 'forgiveness' comes up in the very first session for many of my clients. Over the years I have found that some of the biggest issues that my clients face had their foundation in a lack of forgiveness for themselves or others. It is important to focus on what you are looking to accomplish in forgiving and what you gain in the process. When we go through the pain and hurt and get to the other side, fear is no longer is the ruler … you get to be free.

Forgiveness is not always easy. At times, it feels more painful than the wound we suffered, to forgive the one that inflicted it. And yet, there is no peace without forgiveness. ~Marianne Williamson

In reality, it deeply hurts those who choose not to forgive. When you hold onto the anger, hurt, and resentment that is caused by not forgiving you make it uncomfortable to be with yourself. In that discomfort you may look for something to soothe the beast inside. Alcohol, drugs, and other addictions may ease the pain for a little while, but it never goes away. It stays locked up inside the heart and mind causing a deep unconscious struggle.

Your perception about forgiving is key.

What value does anger and resentment about past actions hold for you?

How do those feelings serve you? You may say that those feelings do not serve you at all … if they didn't you wouldn't still have them. Keep looking deeper into this to find your beliefs. Remember, it is all about you, not what other people have done. You own your space in the world, not being at the effect of other people's stuff.

The weak can never forgive. Forgiveness is the attribute of the strong.

~Mahatma Gandhi

Forgiving creates more comfort with life in so many ways. I have witnessed people in my "Forgive and Let Go" workshop who have experienced powerful physical reactions. Saying things like, 'I feel like bricks have been lifted off my chest,' and "My shoulders are lighter, and I feel freer!"

Forgiveness relieves the hurt; to be clear it does not erase the past, nor does it imply that what happened was okay. When you forgive, what you are saying is that I choose to "let it go" because I love myself and those around me enough to let go of the past and be present to live my greatest life.

Unfortunately, we also hold onto the idea that forgiving is an extremely difficult emotional experience to go through. I believe that it is important to put a lot of attention on compassion to help make it less painful. The suggestion is to forgive the unconscious and flawed thinking of the person/persons who wronged us. Take the time to recognize their ignorance in regard to their thoughts and actions associated with the circumstances. Not always, but much of the time another person's actions were not intentionally meant to hurt you. People are just in their own program of dysfunction and operating from an unconscious place. You choose compassion for the other person's unconscious fear that would make them do what they did. You choose compassion for their unconscious thinking and beliefs. You are not saying that what they did was OK, you are saying that you understand their limited thinking. In that understanding you know that you will no longer allow that kind of behavior or actions to influence you in your life.

Forgiveness also allows us to learn from our experience, to grow from it and gain the wisdom needed to create healthy relationships. We use that information to avoid having to experience the same situation again. When you are looking at the Timeline, many of the patterns that we continue are based in a lack of letting go of the past and carrying it with us. There is focus on the past issue and recreating the event again and again. Not as much focus on the possible fabulous future.

When you don't forgive yourself or others, you have a continual subconscious negative emotional pull on your emotions. When you are holding that kind of negative space in your heart it can make it quite difficult to be fully in love with yourself or someone else. Let's face it, in the scheme of all things, when it comes down to it, LOVE is that thing that makes people want to be present in life.

MIND ROAD TRIP FOR LETTING GO

Take a minute or two and look at your own timeline. Do you see patterns that are happening over and over again? Maybe with relationships? A bad break up with no forgiveness, awareness or understanding? Did you create a similar relationship after that? How about in other areas of your life? Where are you holding onto resentment? Who are you still angry with? Does that situation still matter? Is it worth the feeling that may be holding you down?

GO WITH THE FLOW

Expectations are one of those tricky things in life. We look forward to things in advance of them actually happening and it feels good. Like going on vacation and being excited about all the fun things you are going to do. We get excited about the prospect of a new partner. Getting a new job is usually a big deal. Think about times in your life where you were overly excited for something, and it fell flat. What happened, and how did you feel at the time?

When you are continually in the choice point and holding a clear intention, there is a choice to either resent those things that didn't happen as you wanted them to, or you can *recalibrate* and move into the new direction that life is taking you. I have found over the years that many times it was a blessing that my "plans" didn't happen, and I was able to do something even better.

Remember, your attention is always creative, when life is not just what you expected it is all right to feel disappointment, it's just not a good idea to live in it. Take the time to feel the hurt, then when ready, get back into the flow of life and create with intention. Pay attention to your feelings while driving on the Timeline road of your life.

DRIVE WITH RESILIENCE

I have found time and time again that the people I meet who do not have the ability to deal with challenges as they come up are the ones who "stick their head in the ground" and say that they don't know how to handle the bad news. They get totally involved in the problem, how horrible it is, they will tell anyone who will listen to them about the details of the challenge, and not once focus on what they can do about it. They are simply an unconscious victim to the situations of life. Simply, they don't focus attention on any possible solutions.

Think about the car analogy and the idea of resilience. When you maintain your resilience, you are able to recover as quickly as possible from the drama and traumas of life. You continue to find the next possible solution that will move you up in the Game Board to Cruise Control.

Consider how the car represents the body. For many of us we have to drive our car to get from here to there. Next to our home and phone, it's the most important material thing. If something goes wrong with your car and it will not run, there's just no options, you either have to fix it or you have to get another one. The amount of money that we allocate per month to keep the car maintained and fill with gas is important to note as well. I know for my family it is a chunk of change in the budget. When you take the time to let go of whatever the trauma is, you are owning your power by Be-ing Resilience.

The funny thing is that the *most important thing* is the soul, the driver part of you. We will take our car in to get fixed, but not fix who is driving the car. When you develop your ability to be resilient you make sure that you take your car in for service. Take a pit stop and let someone help to get you back on the road again.

When you own your ability to be resilient, **You Come First**. You are the most important thing. When your tank is full, and you are happy, then everything else can fall into place. It's kind of like when you are on an airplane, and they tell the parents to put on the oxygen first so that you can be there for the kids. I have found in my own life that when I'm happy my household is running smoother, not so much when I let the bothers of the world affect me.

Being resilient means that you keep going, be present in the moment, focus on the solutions and take actions that will move you in the direction of your happiness.

Many people want to be resilient, and they simply just don't know how to do it. They get stuck in the pain of a moment and simply do not know how to move on with life. You may know people who still live as though they were in high school. Or maybe you have a friend who lost a job and feels as though they are incapable of getting another position. In my lifetime I have met many people who talk about the distant past trauma as if it were yesterday. Unfortunately, they have no idea that they are stuck. It is like they are driving off the exit on the freeway and doing the victimization loop to get back onto the same pothole filled freeway.

I had a client that came to me and was so distraught over the end of a marriage. She told me about all the horrible things that he did over and over again, how dishonest, unkind, addicted, etc. Finally, I asked her when this divorce happened, thinking that it was a month ago. She looked me square in the eye and said 8 years ago. Well, I did have a few things to share with her after I heard that.

I told her that it seemed to me the whole time that she was talking that it had just happened as she was so angry and resentful with him. I explained that when we go through something extremely challenging like that, it is important to be in a process to let go of the hurt. In that practice you learn to move into a new direction equipped with the insight and wisdom from lessons learned.

I think that in all those 8 years this had never occurred to her, and understandably so, no one had ever modeled that behavior with her. She came from a strong program of being a victim in life.

My client was able to own her resiliency when…

- ✓ She understood how to own her ability to recognize her behavior and get clarity.
- ✓ She realized that she had been holding on to feelings about something that was long over.
- ✓ She took compassionate responsibility for her part in the relationship and why she stayed.
- ✓ She focused her attention on the intention for her future relationships.
- ✓ She developed a new perception of herself and the value she brings to the world.

In time while continuing the inner work with herself, she was able to change course from her anger, resentment, and remorse. This opened up a new lease on life, and she was able to own her resiliency.

If I were to give being resilient a sound it would be like you have an inner "GURR." There is a lion inside of us that will fight when necessary. Do what works for you to own that inner beast that has your back.

MIND ROAD TRIP FOR RESILIENCE

Ponder your own life for a minute …
Have you had your own share of miserable situations?
How long ago did they happen?
Do you find that you keep creating the same kind of problems?
Do the past problems of your life still cause you to feel hurt or angry?

Did you ever do something constructive to heal from whatever the situation was? Maybe see a therapist, talk it out with a friend or loved? Did you get support in any way? It is a tricky thing getting help for life's problems. We feel like we should know how to fix the hurt, or we should just get over it already, or we think we can just bury it, and it will go away. Could possibly be that a belief in pride might be a factor.

SHIFT INTO THRIVE

- Be in the creative choice point of right now.
- Choose to move forward with conscious intention.
- Feel enthusiasm and excitement.
- Be Mindful of where your Attention is.
- Have Faith in the best and highest happening.
- Use your Creative Imagination to Vision the future.
- Focus on Solutions.
- Take Constructive action.
- Be Resilient.

Once you have done the process with the Timeline and you are securely in the now choice point moment you get to move forward with your intention. You get to really hold that space on the road. The trick is that something may happen with someone that could send you off your path. It's very important to continue to level up your communication skills and own your word.

EFFECTIVE AND CONSTRUCTIVE COMMUNICATION

We usually think that communication, talking with someone is primary about having a conversation with another person, or possibly an animal or thing. The most important conversation that you will ever have is with yourself. Remember, you are the most important thing! So, what does it mean to talk with yourself? In this section you will learn more about your inner communication with yourself, how to communicate better with other people, how to have more of a win/win with relationships, understanding the passengers that we take on and how to deal with them more constructively.

THE BACK-SEAT DRIVER

As you are having a chat with yourself, there are the two that make up you. Your conscious thinking "adult," and the "inner child," whose unconscious beliefs you hold as true. Just as much as you used to be the child in the backseat of your influencer's car, you still have that kid in the backseat of your car … right now. That kid has a lot to say, and you are listening to their chatter a good portion of each day.

How do you know when they have something to say? Are you angry, worried, stressed, or anxious? They are talking. Listen. That is the program and as soon as you recognize it you get to be in the process to change it to what the adult wants.

When I was young, my little Audrey did not get to talk and share what was going on with an adult, so I kept things down and she didn't get a voice. I have learned in all these years to let her have a say in what is going on. I learn from her and more importantly, I heal with her. I communicate and let her know who we are, what we have and that we can do great things in the world.

Are you willing to listen to your little beastie in the back seat?

IT'S ALL ABOUT THE WIN/WIN

I would say that when someone shows up in my office with a problem that they are having with someone else, 95% of the time it is about a lack of good communication. They will sit down and tell me how angry they are with so-and-so, and I will ask them what they said to the person. They look at me like I am crazy and say that they didn't say anything at all to the person that they're angry with. I ask why, and they have said that if they say something, the other person will get mad at them. So, the person in front of me holds the anger, and we now know how creative this is in life.

Let's look at how you not communicating to someone unconsciously creates …

- 😟 The person who did or said whatever does not get to know that their behavior upset you.
- 😟 The other person does not have an opportunity to explain their actions or apologize.
- 😟 They may feel as though something is wrong, but not know what to do about it.
- 😟 On the other hand, you, who did not communicate is now the one who is angry, and you don't have a constructive way to let go of the anger.
- 😟 For both of you, this will not end well.

MIND TRIP FOR CONNECTION

Have you ever had a scenario like this one?

Is there someone who you are angry with that you may want to talk to?

What is your reason for not talking with them?

Have you ever had a friend dump you out of the blue and you never knew why?

Did you ever let someone go without talking with them about why you were letting them go?

Think about all the beliefs that folks have with regard to communication. In their minds the judgements and programming are running the show 24/7.

It can sound like …

- I should not have to tell them, they should know!
- I am too busy; I do not have enough time to talk with them.
- I do not want them to get mad at me.
- I have already told them more than once!
- I just do not know what to say to them.
- It will not matter what I say, they will just do it again.

This list could go on and on. In my 40+ years of working with people, I think I am pretty close to having heard it all! I have also been there done that with my own lack of communication. Remember when I figured out that I could be angry, well, it was a whole other thing to let the person know. That is why I developed this format … it makes it much easier to say what I want to say.

In the picture below you will see the constructive communication format. It is simple, to the point, and wildly effective.

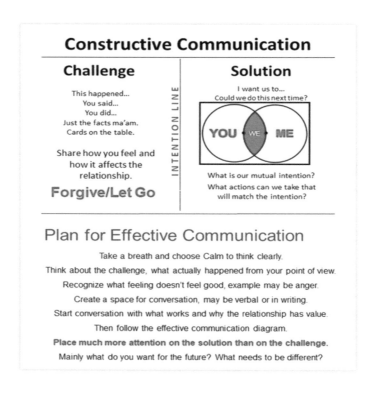

UNSPOKEN COMMUNICATION, THE SILENT DEFINER

We do not usually think about it, but there is a lot of communication that has nothing to do with words. It is in the body language that we're presenting, or those subtle things that we don't even recognize that we're doing.

We communicate to everyone in our lives consciously and unconsciously through body language, our spoken word, what we do not say and what we do say, and we speak volumes in what we do for people, especially our children.

Think about your own life as a child; did your parents do your school projects, did they talk for you, push your coaches to put you in a different position, dress you longer than necessary, etc. Do you do this for your child/children? This is just to ponder and make the necessary adjustments.

TIPS FOR PASSENGERS

Sometimes in our relationships we tend to focus on what the other person is doing. And remember, with our wonderful subconscious programming, much of the time the focus is not on what they are doing right, it's on what we think that they are doing wrong. Stop that! Where attention goes energy flows!

- If you want your relationship to be great, you have to focus on what they are doing that is right.

- Remember how energetically powerful gratitude is? Slather them with appreciation!

- When you are communicating your intention with them it gives them a blueprint on what you both can do for the Win/Win with the relationship.

- A big part of communication is listening, paying attention to what they have to say. One of the things I have clients put on their list for a great future partner is that they are interesting and interested. Be both!

- It is all right to share what your challenges are, just not all the time. Keep the conversation in balance.

- When you want to be supportive, ask, "why, when, what, where or how." Sometimes great communication is about asking and listening.

- Be authentic. Be honest. Lies never seem to have the outcome that we think they will have when we tell them.

- Say things like you would have liked to have heard them.

Great communication does not usually happen overnight. Whether you are talking to yourself or someone else, it's an all day, everyday process of paying attention to your feelings, thoughts and words. Use your feelings to guide you, use your thoughts to understand and your words to own your power in a constructive manner.

THE VICTIMIZATION LOOP

MOVING FROM VICTIM TO VALUABLE

There is a strong tendency for people to not want to accept the "blame" for what has happened. It was someone else that caused this, certainly not me! I had nothing to do with it. They took advantage, they lied, they did whatever, and I was but a mere victim to the circumstances.

I know this one … really well! I spent many years being the victim in many crazy situations. Not fun! When I finally understood what I am about to tell you, everything changed, and I got off of my dysfunctional victimization loop.

To begin, it is you, EVERYTHING is always about you.

Think about it, people will do what they do, and in the scheme of things, it always comes back to *you*. Consider all aspects of the victimization loop with compassion, this is a soul-searching process, and it takes all the consciousness you can muster to work through this with grace. Remember you are changing the unhealthy beliefs and ideas. You are literally owning a new way of being. If you genuinely want to create change that will move you in the right direction, you have to know why the past happened in the first place. You are the common denominator in all the situations that have happened to you. Sometimes it truly is that someone has done something to you, in this exercise you are looking at your response, the attention you placed on the details, what actions you took in moving forward. In this process you are recognizing your limiting beliefs to bring them to the surface for constructive change.

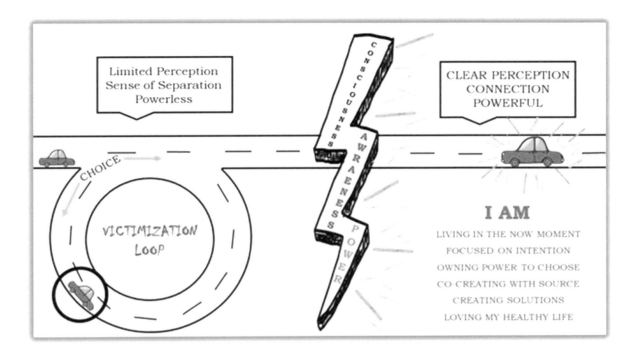

When you choose to take responsibility for your actions and choices, it makes it easier to let things go. You are owning your power to learn from your past unconscious choices and set the boundaries of what you will allow in the future. When you avoid the Victimization Loop, you make a choice point to use all the tools you have gained. You hold a new space for yourself on the road.

MIND TRIP FOR GETTING OFF THE LOOP

Ponder these questions and remember this is designed to help you move off the victimization loop and onto the freeway of your greatest dreams. If there is something that is still holding space in your heart and mind that doesn't feel good, maybe this exercise will help you "dump the trunk" and let it go. Remember when you are taking responsibility for any of it, it doesn't make you wrong or bad. Whatever we did in the past was with our old consciousness, this is to bring about a clean slate with new awareness and new choices.

- The choices that you made in the first place.
  - You chose to be with them, you said yes to the job, you agreed to do that thing, etc.
- The choices that kept you in the situation.
  - You chose to stay, you chose to leave, you chose to ignore their behavior, you chose to give them more than enough chances, etc.

What you choose to do with regard to their actions.
  - You chose not to say anything, say too much, you chose to let them do what you did not want them to do, etc.
- Did you communicate clearly and effectively?
- Did you feel like there were no other options?
- Did you set your boundaries?
- Did you hold those boundaries?

TALKING TO MYSELF AND FEELING DOWN

When you find yourself having that negative self-talk about how things do not seem to go your way, or maybe people always do _____ to you. When you are thinking about anything that may make yourself seem like a victim to your circumstances, be aware. That would be the time to remember that you have the power to change your circumstances in some way or another. It may not be exactly what you want at this very moment. It is OK, line the car up in the direction you desire, stay focused on driving on your conscious side of the road. Keep In mind that you are greater than your immediate body, and that you have a bubble of immunity.

THE BUBBLE OF IMMUNITY

Well, now you have taken responsibility for your life, and you're holding that space on the road. Consider creating a bubble of immunity for yourself.

If you were to think of this with the car analogy, it is a force field that surrounds the car. It protects the car, and you, the driver. For many of us, we drive a car daily. The heavy metal and airbags protect us from the elements and many kinds of danger a good amount of the time.

When you are creating your personal bubble of immunity you are creating an energetic bubble around you and holding a space to be "protected from other people's negativity." This is where you own a power statement that says, *"I am immune to your negativity, it doesn't serve me."* Or *"that's their business, not mine."* Take time to think about what power statements would work for you. Hold that thought, and imagine yourself in your bubble, immune to the chaos and negativity around you.

To be clear, this does not mean that we ignore the world around us and think that we're separate from other people. It means that we are choosing to be calm about what is going on around us to that we can think clearly and focus on the solutions. We aren't' getting caught up in the problem, we're focused on what we can do that will move things in the direction of peace, compassion, abundance, love, cooperation, etc.

I am not saying that this is the easiest thing to do, it takes patience, practice, and perseverance. The more you use your Bubble of Immunity, the more life is on your terms, and you create from your own feelings, thoughts, and intentions. You are not at the effect of the world. You create from your own center of your world.

MIND TRIP FOR RELATIONSHIPS

Look at the diagram below and then ask yourself the questions.

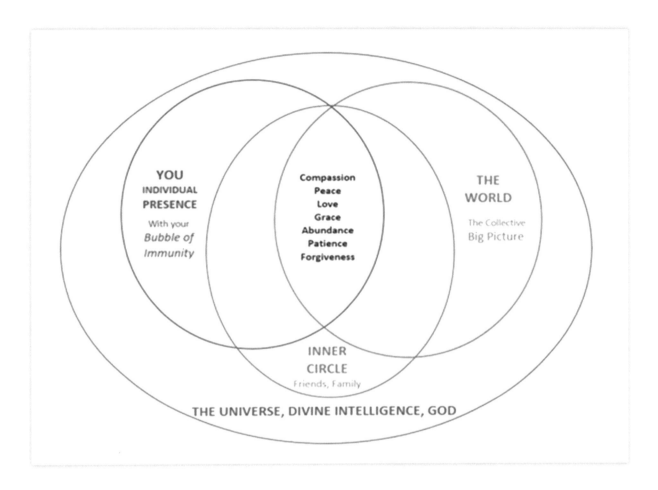

∞ Relationships have an impact, notice where you are in relation to:
- o Your own Mental, Emotional and Physical Self
- o Divine Intelligence, God, Universe
- o Your Inner Circle
- o The World

∞ Is the environment around you working in your favor or against you?

∞ How much of what happens around you has an effect that takes you off your path of peace?

∞ Focus your attention on what you know to be true, the desired outcome, and on the solutions.

BE THE MOST VALUABLE PLAYER

M ★ V ★ P

MEDITATION   VISUALIZATION   PRAYER

I learned how to pray through the church, they did not teach meditation or visualization. They said ask God of things, and he will grant it to you if you only believe, and, if you have been a good girl. It didn't take long for that to be added to the pile of things that I was disillusioned about. God certainly was not granting me anything I was begging for, he probably noticed that I wasn't being so good. My wicked ways had cut me out of the grace of God.

So, for years I did not pray. I had no spiritual practice what-so-ever, and my life was the epitome of dysfunction. I had a friend direct me to Agape International Spiritual Center, where I was finally able to create a strong spiritual practice. It was not easy at first, Meditation and Prayer were incredibly challenging for me. I just could not sit still and clear my oh so busy mind. Over time I have developed my own approach to meditation and prayer that works for me. My favorite is when I get out in nature to walk, dance and daydream. I get into the energy of the earth and vibe with everything good.

MEDITATION

TURN ON THE HEADLIGHTS

There is this idea that we are just here in this little human body and all we can see is what we know and what is presented to us. When you meditate is gives you the ability to see more clearly the world around you, outside of the car. So, when you take the time to connect it is like you are turning on the headlights and the interior light to see better what's in the darkness.

- ∞ The word meditation means to become familiar with, in this context it's that you are getting familiar with the higher part of you, Universal Intelligence.
- ∞ In meditation you are connected with source Intelligence. You're recognizing "I Am **THAT** I Am."

∞ It is a time to turn off the mind and let the unconscious chatter be silent and listen to the higher part of you.

∞ When you are meditating you are emptying your mind and allowing.

∞ You are opening up your mind and body to source energy.

∞ Sometimes meditation will create a physical sensation.

When I personally have a "rush," I get a massive vibration of what I can only call, Life Force Energy … honestly, there is not a word for describing it. It feels amazing, expansive, full, complete, turned on, pleasant, peaceful. My body vibrates, and it makes my eyes water. In meditation I am in the flow, and it is like a beam of light going through the spinal column and into every channel in my body. It feels like the biggest happiness, the grandest love, deepest peace, in a connected to everything kind of way. As an example, when I go into the woods on a "Soulitude," it is a lot of meditation for most of the time that I'm gone. I hardly say very many words, and I'm in a position of *allowing* for Intelligence to communicate with and through me. I am in a point of *being* and *accepting* … not doing.

I have found that being in nature is an excellent way to reclaim your connection with your higher power. There is not the usual distraction of our internet lives, no energetic frequencies that are unlike nature, and the earth is very calming with grounding energy. You may want to try going to any area in nature that feels good for you. Try sitting with your shoes off and taking in all of the elements around you.

That is my favorite form of meditation, your task is to experiment and test drive different approaches that will work for you. There are many ways to bring about the experience, try some groups in your community, try online sources or use apps with the modality that may work the best for you. I have guided meditations that you may find useful on my website and Tools for Transformation Podcast.

Keep going with it, meditation is a practice, the more you do it the more it will be natural, effortless, and expansive.

VISIONING

LIMITLESS DESTINATION

Like I said at the beginning of the book, you get to create from conscious intention or unconscious consequences. When you intentionally hold a vision for your life with Source Intelligence and then take constructive actions miracles will happen in your life.

So, what does that mean a vision, or for that matter, what exactly is Visioning?

Visualization is seeing within your mind the things that you want to have, what you want to accomplish or any intention for your future. An example is to visualize yourself having that great relationship, that successful job, that dream vacation and those little details of a great life. For me, completing this book and all the blessings that it will bring has been a great avenue for my vision.

My editor mentioned that I could share with you the relationship between daydreaming and visualization, or if there is a difference between an idle dreaming and a visualization. I would say that visualization is more intentional and directed to a specific purpose or something that you would like to manifest. Daydreaming is just letting your mind wander to anything that might feel good. It would be like going on a road trip with no destination, just letting your spontaneity lead the way. I did that once with my girls… what an adventure!

With Visioning, you allow for the connection with Universal Intelligence and be open to receive the unlimited possibilities for your best and highest to happen. When you practice Visioning you are creating a human awareness of your greatest destination. When you do this process, it creates an ability for you to see in your mind's eye the possibilities for an optimal path to take. Armed with that information, you are able to establish a mental equivalent, a new neural pathway in your brain … New Thinking. This will then give you the ability to map out your course.

With visioning it's like telling the Universe that you would love to have some leading road signs to give you direction to your best and highest happening.

The process of visioning is like a mixture of meditation and visualization. You get still and in a state of allowing, but then you are asking questions, knowing that the answers are being shared with you. I believe that these questions are personal to each of us, so come up with questions for yourself prior to your Visioning. Below I am sharing some basic questions that may be helpful for you.

MIND TRIP FOR VISIONING

- ★ What is the best and highest vision for my love life?
- ★ What vision equals success with career, education, earnings, etc. look like?
- ★ What would be the best way to create more abundance?
- ★ What is the vision for my healthiest body?
- ★ What is the greatest vision for my happiness?
- ★ What must I become to empower the vision?
- ★ What must I let go of?
- ★ What must I embrace?
- ★ What actions can I take to manifest this vision?

Have a notepad handy for those inspired thoughts. If you find yourself judging, take that to the Fear Into Power exercise. Keep redirecting your thoughts, your car and your feelings into the Vision that is presented.

PURPOSE FULL PRAYER

I had such a time with prayer when I was first learning all this information, and to be honest, it is one of my practices that I've had to continually remind myself to do. I have been thinking about it a lot and pondering on why praying would be such a chore for me. On my last trip I took the time to look back into my childhood and figure out what that unconscious program is. What I realized is that in my youth I was not encouraged to ask for help, and I was told specifically to not take help when offered. I was taught that if you wanted something you had to be the one to earn it, no handouts. Asking was setting myself up for not getting much of the time. So, you can see the program running and why would I have trouble asking. When I was learning about prayer at Agape Spiritual Center, I thought it was an asking kind of thing. Actually, I thought that for many years! Thank goodness I finally understood what a purposeful prayer really is, and how to fully embrace my ability to use the power of prayer.

This purposeful kind of prayer is not even really asking, it's more of a connection, declaration and allowing process. Ernest Holmes's teachings were the foundation for this kind of prayer, and Gregg Braden has taken that to the next level.

Through the art of affirmative prayer, the limitless resources of the Spirit are at my command. The power of the Infinite is at my disposal. ~Ernest Holmes

When prayer removes distrust and doubt and enters the field of mental certainty, it becomes faith; and the universe is built on faith. ~Ernest Holmes

Prayer is a thought, a belief, a feeling, arising within the mind of the one praying. ~Ernest Holmes

The secret of our lost mode of prayer is to shift our perspective of life by feeling that the miracle has already happened, and our prayers have been answered. Now we have the opportunity to bring this wisdom into our lives as prayers of gratitude for what already exists, rather than asking for our prayers to be answered.
~Gregg Braden

DESTINATION SET

There is a format for the type of prayer that I have learned, and I really find it valuable to use. There are five stages to it, and an excellent reason to use those stages. In these stages you will see where they come from in the prior chapters.

One of the most important things to remember in this kind of prayer is that it is not as much in the words as it is in the feeling of the prayer. Think back to the heart/brain connection. The brain is putting out the request in the intentional statements and the heart is talking to the Intelligence to put the request into the field of energy that you are driving into.

5 STAGES OF PRAYER

1. Energy, Intelligence, Matrix
   I am recognizing the intelligent energy that is everywhere present.
2. I Am THAT I Am
   Divine Intelligence flows through me as me, I Am THAT I Am.
3. Power Statement in Action
   My intentions are in action right now.
4. Thank You, It is Happening!
   I appreciate EVERYTHING!
5. I Let It Be

My faith leads the way to my greatest and highest happening.

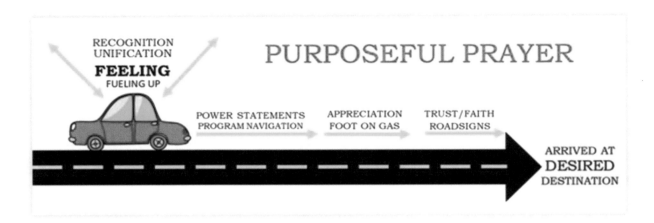

Over the years I have written some of my prayers down for people to give an example. This Intentional Living Prayer is a great one to hold close to your heart. I have used this many times in my own moments of distress and challenge, it has really helped to realign my feelings and thoughts. More importantly it brings me back to "home." The deep connection with my higher self, that God connection.

INTENTIONAL LIVING PRAYER

I recognize that we live in a vast limitless sea of intelligent energy, a divine matrix. This energy is receptive to me, and I create within it. I access knowledge and access my infinite power through this Universal Mind. I pray from a place of recognizing that this powerful, co-creative energy is the I Am That I Am.

I am one with the creative intelligence of the Universe. I allow myself to be fully connected with, and as this greater power. I am fully present to this divine energy as it flows in and as me; it is the intelligence that I consciously use to create my human experience.

Divine right action is always taking place in my life. Peace and calm are the order of this day. I live in love, knowing that my intelligence and wisdom guide me toward creating even more intentionally. I constantly say Yes to happiness, Yes to abundance, Yes to clarity, and Yes to moving forward in my life on purpose! I consciously own a truth that is powerful. I do this all with ease and grace.
I stand buoyed in my faith, knowing that all things are happening with my highest and best taking place.

I appreciate that I am creating something wonderful for myself. I am grateful to have the willingness and the ability to recreate my life from greater intention. I feel so good to know that I live in a supportive universe and that all is well.
I stand in these words of truth, knowing that it is done, and I allow it to Be.
And so it is ... Amen.

I highly recommend that you create your own rhythm of meditation, visualization, and prayer. Experiment with different approaches to see what will fit your personality and lifestyle. Go to the YouTube link for more information on this one ... seriously I could talk for days about this subject.

BALANCE AND ALIGNMENT

THE WHEELS IN YOUR LIFE GO ROUND AND ROUND

This is one of those things that many of us do not even realize that we're doing. We tend to lean into one specific area of life and get out of balance and alignment. As an example, many people are "workaholics" and spend way too much time climbing the business ladder, while others are virtually gaming to excess and live almost non present in their human reality, and there are those of us who become fixated on health and spend an inordinate amount of focus on exercise, eating and health issues. It seems like that wouldn't be a problem as it is about health and wellbeing, but like anything else it can go into becoming obsessed with one area of life and ignoring the others. What is your deal? For this week, notice how you are spending your time and where your attention is.

There is always going to be some kind of contrast in our life. There will be those times that everything is at least all right, up to wildly happy, in love and exuberant. We will call it the High Road. Then, there will be those moments of challenge, despair, grief, and sadness. Those are the moments where there is an opportunity to use the momentum to lift up your life, to see the place that you can go to overcome the fear and move into your power. Life needs movement, and it will get that movement one way or another. Think of the wheel of life in the diagram above, if there is no movement we just stay where we are, the key is to know when to use the struggle to go in the direction of your dreams, not your nightmares. You have an opportunity to choose.

MIND TRIP FOR ALIGNMENT AND BALANCE

Take a minute and map out the time you spend "doing" in your life.
What can you change to gain more balance?
It is a process to balance life … for some of you it may be the first time you have gone about the business of creating balance ever.
Take time to create your own center and focus on what you want.
There will be greater success, better health, deeper love, and joy.

THE ROAD CONTINUES

Well, you have reached the end of this book, and the beginning of a new experience in your life. Kudos for all your effort!

This is a good time to look at how far you have come on your journey. Take time to think about how you were driving your car when you started this Mind Trip. Take time to look back at the notes that you made in the Fear to Power notebook. What new pathways have you created in your mind? How much better do you feel emotionally, mentally, and physically? Do you have less drama happening? For many of us it takes time, you did not get to be how you were overnight, it is a process of change. Each time around the gameboard of life will continually bring you closer to greater happiness.

I have a program that I offer to clients, it's a 5-session package, and usually they come once a week. I have found that many of my clients don't even realize how much change has happened in a mere five weeks, and once I point it out to them, they are rather surprised. Have you noticed that you've changed? How?

This was not designed to be a "do this" for however many weeks. It is a program for the rest of your life. There will always be that next thing that will challenge you and cause you to have to stop the car and figure out what to do. The good news is that when you do figure it out it equals and better and better life for you and your loved ones. So, keep leveling up and being that greater version of you!

Now, for your last Mind Trip, take the time to write down what actions you can take to continue moving yourself forward. Each day is a new day to determine who you will choose to be. Put this list up where you will be able to see it first thing in the morning and choose one thing to focus on that will help you drive your day with conviction, courage, and creativity.

Here are some suggestions.

- ∞ Put a reminder on your phone to take five during the day to refocus.
- ∞ Take time to go outside and put your feet on the earth to be grounded.
- ∞ Make new food choices that support a healthy lifestyle.
- ∞ Call an old friend to reconnect.
- ∞ Clean out useless items in your home.
- ∞ Make a vision board.
- ∞ Join up with a new form of exercise.
- ∞ Meetup with new like-minded people.
- ∞ Watch a video that will inspire you.
- ∞ Play with a child or animal that makes you feel happy.
- ∞ Go outside at night and watch the stars.
- ∞ Do something that makes you feel brave.
- ∞ Tell someone how much you appreciate them.
- ∞ Take a calming bath.
- ∞ Play a game with friends.
- ∞ Meditate in a new way.
- ∞ Organize one closet.
- ∞ Be of service to the world.

The suggestion is to add to this list on a regular basis. Make some of the actions fun, and some that are more on the challenging side. Remember that you will get closer to your destination when you push yourself a bit to step out of your old habits.

END OF THE ROAD FOR NOW

Well, it has been quite a journey writing this book and sharing my road with you. I have grown immensely in this process, seriously, this was one of my greatest challenges to this point. Thank goodness I had my tools to help me when I lost my courage, when I became distracted, when I didn't feel trusting of myself, and when I created too much of a busy life to be present with it. I chose to own my brave, my focus, my faith and my ability to be present and persevere. It was all worth it for this moment of being complete, this book is done.

Now you have your own Toolbox and new resources to help guide you on the road. I wish you well on your journey, may light and love lead your way to your greatest destinations. Continue to know how powerful you are, expand your horizons, lead with love, and drive with the Universe leading the way.

Much Love to you!
Audrey

DEEP APPRECIATION TO THOSE ON MY JOURNEY

First acknowledgement would be to the #1 driver, God, Divine Source Intelligence… Everything that I have said in this book is with Spirit leading the way. Words can't describe the feelings that come up as I feel gratitude for this guidance.

I am also beyond grateful to all my teachers along the way, Golden Arrow/Alexandra, you have continued to show me the path, starting with my first "Soulitude" trip and up to this one right now… I did see the magic on this trip!

Merlin/Nick Newmont, Abraham/Ester Hicks, The Guides/Paul Selig, and Joseph/Michael G. Reccia, all of you have such a powerful message for humanity! I am so happy I listened to your insights and wisdom. Your words have been a foundation for all that I do.

To all the teachers who have quotes in this book, each of you has been an excellent source of information and I wouldn't have been able to have written any of this had it not been for you leading the way. My deepest appreciation to all of you!

To all my clients along the way, thank you so much for trusting me with your challenges and allowing me to be a source of new information, insight, compassion, wisdom, new tools, and love. You have greatly helped me to go deeper into my own personal practice, and therefore deeper into my own consciousness. It has been a beautiful gift to watch you all gain more of your joy, success, abundance, health and love in your life!

To all my friends who have been there for me through all these years, thanks for your patience with my pontificating, compassion when I was down, your support in my endeavors, and your love that has been a source of strength. I love you all.

To my family, I love you all very much and I appreciate your love for me greatly. You are all a foundation for so many things in my life, and I am blessed to call you, my home.

To my daughters, words are not enough to describe how much I love each of you. You have all been an enormous part of my personal growth, and I certainly wouldn't be me without you! It has been my greatest joy to bring you all into the world and enjoy the delightful relationships with you all. Thank you all for being there for me as it has taken all these years of me working on this while away from you.

Finally, and very important, a huge THANK YOU to my wonderful husband, and life partner Nick. You have always said yes and have supported me from day one on this journey. I appreciate all your advice and the parts of the book that you have inspired and shared with me… like the Victimization Loop. I love having you in the front seat for all these 25 years!

Printed in the United States
by Baker & Taylor Publisher Services